D0571759

PRAISE FOR *THUMBS UP!*

"*Thumbs Up!* is terrific—Joey's best book ever. When you read it, it will change your perspective on how to best live your life and give you a hand in finding your personal purpose."

—Carol Tomé, CFO, Home Depot

"In reading *Thumbs Up!*, I felt as if I were a student earmarking pages so that I could easily reference important ideas.

However, I found myself earmarking each page. Whether a story or a quote, each page contains ideas and principles that inspire, reinforcing the importance of finding our own individual purpose.

Thumbs Up! has made me reflect on who I am and inspired me to recommit to who I want to be . . . and bring it to life every day. More importantly, I'm confident every reader of *Thumbs Up!* will experience a similar sense of excitement about her/his purpose and serve as a fantastic role model for many others to follow their dreams and live happier lives.

Now, it's time for me to work on my 'forgettory.' When you read the book, you'll know how important this can be!"

—Neil Golden, former CMO, McDonald's

"I met Joey Reiman when he was creating Master Ideas for companies needing a fresh inspiration. I enjoyed his book on Purpose because so many people and companies never gave thought to their Purpose. And now Joey inspires us with his 'Thumbs Up' attitude toward life that he illustrates with many unforgettable stories. If you are seeking greater purpose in your life, seek out this gem."

—PHILIP KOTLER, professor of marketing at the Kellogg School of Management and author of *Winning Global Markets and Confronting Capitalism*

"Great social movements have always depended on individuals standing up and living out their fundamental hope that people and circumstances can change. Joey Reiman explores techniques and approaches required to inspire and sustain individual leaders on the journey of leadership. This book outlines powerful approaches to unlocking the potential within each of us."

—DOUG SHIPMAN, founding CEO, National Center for Civil and Human Rights

"From the boardroom to the bedroom, purpose brings meaning and value. Joey's newest book shines the light on living optimistically."

—JAY GOULD, COO, Interface

"Capturing success is easier than capturing happiness, but Joey Reiman once again plots a course for those of us looking for an authentic and wise guide through this crazy world. With his help we can have both. High five."

—Hugh Acheson, chef, author, and judge on *Top Chef*

"Time never stops for us. And when it does, we find ourselves at the proverbial crossroad of life. Some of us are not as lucky. We keep doing what we do and never reflect on what we should do.

Joey Reiman's book *Thumbs Up!* gives us a magical 'Time Out in Life.' It provides a path to create and bring meaningful purpose to what we do and how we do it. I loved the fact that I found hope in its pages and a substantial deposit into our personal account we call faith.

When an athlete goes down, a hand always appears out of nowhere to pull the athlete up. Joey Reiman is that hand for all of us who have fallen down.

Joey has taken purpose and puts it front and center. He took purpose and brought meaning to business. Now he takes purpose and brings meaning to life in a way that is mesmerizing and energizing. One thing is for sure, you will never look at a hand or fingers the same way."

—William A. Burke, III, COO, Newell Rubbermaid

"Why merely survive when you can thrive. Joey Reiman knows how to translate the hard questions into palatable actions. Never has the quest for meaning been so central and elusive. But, hold *Thumbs Up!* in your hands and you'll be one step closer to finding purpose in all corners of your life."

—ESTHER PEREL, leading relationship therapist and speaker

"The lessons learned in this book are timeless and applicable to anyone. Reiman teaches his students to keep a 'Thumbs Up' attitude and now everyone, with the help of this book, can learn how your hand can serve as your handbook to success."

—ERIKA JAMES, dean of Emory University Goizueta Business School

"Joey Reiman's *Thumbs Up!* is a remarkable book of his recovery from a devastating injury and the universal lessons he learned as he struggled back from an uncertain fate. *Thumbs Up!* is a positive and powerful guide I use to encourage my patients to have faith in their ability to heal and thrive! If someone needs a helping hand—I strongly recommend *Thumbs Up!*."

—CRAIG WEIL, MD, orthopedic hand surgeon

"*Thumbs Up!* is that rare combination of a book that is at once profound and playful, wise and joyful. It will put air beneath your wings, ground under your feet, and give you a map that will help you find the purpose of your life. Read it and delight . . ."

—SAM KEEN, philosopher and author of *Fire in the Belly*

"When you thumb through the pages of *Thumbs Up!*, you find yourself searching for the story of your own personal purpose. Joey shows us how success is in our hands and that giving the world and yourself a thumbs up can put you on the path to a happier life, and when you give others a thumbs up, it can create a movement for a happier world. Thank you, Joey, for reminding us that life is in the details because it is a detail we often forget. Thumbs Up!"

—US SENATOR MAX CLELAND (Ret.)

"Joey honestly and passionately believes that the only certainty is that any given moment must be lived to the fullest. He has devoted his professional life to helping companies maximize potential by finding purpose and creating meaning in the world. His new book helps individuals do the same. Thumbs up!!"

—ANDREA HERSHATTER, senior associate dean of Undergraduate Education, Emory University Goizueta Business School

"This book deserves two thumbs up. Every parent should buy this book to read to their children. Joey takes one of his life lessons and turns it into lessons for a better life."

—COREY KEYES, professor of sociology and the Winship Distinguished Research Professor at Emory University

THUMBS UP!

THUMBS UP!

FIVE STEPS TO CREATE
THE LIFE OF YOUR DREAMS

JOEY REIMAN

BenBella Books, Inc.
Dallas, Texas

BenBella Books, Inc.
10300 N. Central Expressway
Suite #530
Dallas, TX 75231
www.benbellabooks.com
Send feedback to feedback@benbellabooks.com

Printed in the United States of America
10 9 8 7 6 5 4 3 2 1

Library of Congress Cataloging-in-Publication Data
Reiman, Joey.
   Thumbs up! : five steps to create the life of your dreams / by Joey Reiman.
        pages cm
   Includes bibliographical references and index.
   ISBN 978-1-941631-19-5 (trade cloth : alk. paper) — ISBN 978-1-941631-20-1 (ebook) 1. Optimism. 2. Success—Psychological aspects. I. Title.
   BF698.35.O57R45 2015
   158.1—dc23

                                        2014049828

Editing by Vy Tran
Copyediting by James Fraleigh
Proofreading by Cameron Proffitt and Kimberly Broderick
Cover design by Sarah Dombrowsky
Cover thumb icon designed by Freepik
Text design by Silver Feather Design
Text composition by PerfecType, Nashville, TN
Printed by Lake Book Manufacturing

Distributed by Perseus Distribution
www.perseusdistribution.com

To place orders through Perseus Distribution:
Tel: (800) 343-4499
Fax: (800) 351-5073
E-mail: orderentry@perseusbooks.com

Significant discounts for bulk sales are available. Please contact Glenn Yeffeth at glenn@benbellabooks.com or (214) 750-3628.

Dedicated to Cynthia, who gave me her hand in marriage, and to our sons, Alden and Julien, who will shape the world with their hands.

"We do not see things as they are.
We see things as we are."
—*The Talmud*

CONTENTS

FOREWORD

I AGREED TO WRITE THIS FOREWORD because the author, Joey Reiman, is moving the world forward.

My grandfather, Mohandas Karamchand "Mahatma" Gandhi, taught me a simple concept that impacted my life and many lives around the world. He said, "Be the change you wish to see in the world." That one thought has traveled around the globe and back. He lived that thought and inspired millions. I live his words and his ideals every day and continue to help put them into action. I also know there is still so much work to do.

Joey Reiman is helping me do this work. In his new book, *Thumbs Up,* Reiman espouses the power of looking up. This one idea has a universal power to impact us all. Grandfather looked up and spent his life lifting the spirits and souls of some of the most disadvantaged and underserved populations on earth.

Joey Reiman helps us lift our spirits as well. He invites us to do one simple thing—to raise our consciousness and look to possibility. To create a plan, take action, and make our lives and the lives of others better one day at a time. In a no-nonsense style, he teaches us that even problems are opportunities. It's all about how you see the world from where you are standing. Regardless of where or who you are, Reiman's practical lessons will brighten that view. As Grandfather said, "If I have the belief that I can do it, I shall surely acquire the capacity to do it, even if I may not have it at the beginning."

Today, I bring you a mandate: Create a positive presence in the world. Personally take charge of your actions and change greed, anger, frustration, and other negative attitudes into love, respect, understanding, compassion, and acceptance.

We have the ability to live positive lives and project ourselves as powerful, purposeful people doing more good for more people in more places. As my grandfather said, "The best way to find yourself is to lose yourself in the service of others."

This transformation will take acts of love from each of us. Love is still and always will be the basis of civilization. Can we become this change we wish to see in the world?

I join my ancestors and Joey Reiman in answering with a resounding YES. By believing in the human spirit and ourselves, we will unlock our true potential. It begins with one thumb, one thought, and one person thinking it is possible. Be the change you wish to see in yourself.

Move forward with me as I follow in my grandfather's footsteps to inspire and engage others in meaningful, purposeful, and lasting societal change by taking the world into our own hands.

Thumbs Up,

—**ARUN GANDHI**

Founder/President

Gandhi Worldwide Education Institute, Wauconda, IL

http://www.gandhiforchildren.org

THE THUMBS UP LETTER THAT INSPIRED ME TO WRITE THIS BOOK

A FATHER GAVE MY ORIGINAL BOOK on success, written approximately twenty years ago, to his son, which changed his life. Last year, his son sent me the open letter below, which shares a personal story of how giving someone a thumbs up can come in different forms. After learning of my impact on his life, I was so humbled that I wrote this book. I call that the full circle and the power of Thumbs Up.

—JOEY REIMAN

It's a long story, but here goes: When Joey was running the Joey Reiman Agency in the early to mid-1990s (before what we'd now call a pivot into the idea consultancy), his offices were in Buckhead Plaza, which is where my dad, Sylvain Lidsky, ran the shoe-repair store on the ground floor, Buckhead Plaza Shoe Service. Joey was a customer of my dad's. At some point, around late 1993, Joey gave my dad a first edition of his inspirational self-help book called *Success: The Original Handbook.*

It took me a while to get around to reading it, but as they say, sometimes you don't read a book until you're ready for it. I read it when I was flailing about trying to figure out what I was going to do with my life. I'd gone to law school, but I had no passion for a career as a lawyer. Law firms knew it, too, and I couldn't even get an interview for a job I'd hate. For six months following graduation I was an associate at a discount department store chain making $6 an hour—not the kind of professional associate my dad had in mind! Then I moved back home with my folks. At age twenty-five, overeducated and under-skilled, I was a cliché— a subspecies of the then much-discussed Generation X.

Joey's book really helped my attitude and gave me a framework to focus on what I might want to do and how to make it happen. And then Joey generously agreed to meet me. It was the spring of 1995. Advertising was one of the arenas that interested me (along with journalism), and Joey was very supportive and encouraging. He told me he'd give me a job if he had one to give me (which may have been a cold offer, but it certainly gave me hope), and he told me a bit of advice that has held up amazingly well: If all you care about is making money, you'll end up making money. But if you do what you love, maybe you won't make any money early on, but in the end you'll do all right.

Perhaps a month after I met with Joey, I moved back to New York City, which is where I wanted to be. Two months later, after a few false starts, I got my foot in the door at *PC Magazine*, which was then the largest and most successful magazine of any kind. I was a freelance fact checker and really liked it. They had entry-level job openings and after a few weeks of freelancing they asked me to think about taking a full-time position. The salary was $21,000. My law-school loans would swallow up 50 percent of my take-home pay; rent would take the rest. I was scared to death to take this job. I spent a weekend despairing about the offer and how I'd swing it. But I remembered Joey's words of advice. And I decided to go for it.

It obviously paid off. I got promoted twice in sixteen months, which got me to a more livable wage. (For years, in a tribute designed for my own personal enjoyment, I closed every email I wrote with "Thumbs Up.") Today, I have what my wife calls "the last good job in journalism," and I love it more now, nineteen years later, than I did when I first thrilled to full-time employment in the field. I am arguably the most successful journalist from my college class, even though I never worked on the school paper or took any courses in its vaunted journalism grad school. And it all started

when Joey gave my dad a copy of his book for me
and when he agreed to meet the son of the guy
who ran a service business in his building. Think
about that. I can't even formulate a commensurate
equivalent in my life.

—**DAVID LIDSKY**
Deputy Editor, *Fast Company*

PROLOGUE

LET'S START WITH A HANDSHAKE. YOU take my hand and I'll help you create the life you have always dreamed about.

"I Want to Hold Your Hand" was the Beatles' first hit, and today the best electronic device is still a handheld. The brain reaches out to the hand and the hand reaches out to the world.

The hand has its hand in everything. Being hands on excites us; being hands off incites us. "All hands on deck" is a call for help. "Biting the hand that feeds you" is called betrayal. To know someone firsthand is an act of caring. To force someone's hand is an act of daring.

Having a free hand liberates you; being hand-cuffed is arresting. To gain the upper hand is to have control, and to get your hands dirty is to have a task. To give a hand is to help. To give a guiding hand is to give hope. They usually go hand in hand.

To be in good hands is to be safe. A hand-me-down is saved. We work hand over fist to make a living. We hand in our best work when we work hand in glove.

Every day we hand something off, something on, something out, and something over. We might even hand something to someone on a silver platter.

When you are appreciated you will hear, "I have to hand it to you." When we are exhausted we say our hands are full. To be an old hand is an honor. To play into someone's hands is dishonor. To wash your hands of something is to throw in the towel, but when one hand washes the other we have community.

If only we were all on hand, the world wouldn't be so out of hand and underhanded. We would not throw our hands up, be heavy handed, or overplay our hand. Many people would not be living hand to mouth and taking the law into their own hands. Often it appears that the left hand does know what the right hand is doing. God only knows that the devil makes work for idle hands.

On the other hand, if we were to take a show of hands, most of us would take someone by the hand and get to know them like the back of our hand. We would move from a put-your-hands-up world to a raise-your-hand society where we all ask just one question: How can I lend a hand?

Answer that, and you'll have the whole world in your hands.

THUMBS UP!

INTRODUCTION

THE AGE OF INSPIRATION

I have ended all of my books with my favorite mantra: *THANK GOD FOR GOD*. This one begins with it, because if I have learned anything in my sixty years, it's that if you believe in something greater than yourself, you will create the greatest self you can be.

All you need is a hands-on approach in order to live a really meaningful and successful life. In fact, success is right at your fingertips and in your hands.

I define true success as waking up excited and going to bed feeling safe. There are thousands of handbooks available on success but only one is attached to your arm—the only one you can count on. It's your hand. God gave us hands to hold what is dear, grab what is exciting, and pick up what is needed. Whether those objects are love, money, or health, this little book will show you how everything you have ever dreamed of is right at your fingertips.

In 1986, I was asked to give a speech in Tampa, Florida, to a crowd of five hundred people. As a former ad guy, I was going around the world sharing my message that we are walking ads for ourselves. The image we create changes the way people look at us and act toward us. Like most advertisements, we, too, have headlines, visuals, copy, and unique selling propositions.

I inspired generations of people to ask the simple question, "What is your headline?" Positive advertising sells positively, and nobody wants to buy a negative image. I offered insight into how to sell the most important product in the world . . . you! I called it *Youvertising*.

When I landed in Tampa, my driver commented on how much he loved a speech I gave years ago called "You Are an Ad." *Oh no!* The moment I heard that, I realized that this audience was the exact audience who had already heard my speech a year ago. Panic took over. My mind was racing. The river below the bridge we were passing looked like a better alternative than the embarrassment I would face by delivering the identical speech. With two hours until show time, I had to write a brand new talk.

I checked into the hotel, walked out onto my room's veranda, looked out to the heavens, and asked myself, *Why am I here? What is my purpose?*

Mark Twain wrote that the two most important days of your life are the day you are born and the day you find out why. This was to become my *why* day.

Suddenly a date came to my mind—June 11, 1975—the day I was nearly killed in a car crash in Rome, Italy. Was that accident the reason I was here?

HOW I TURNED A MESS INTO MY MESSAGE

While recuperating in an Italian hospital, I had learned five lessons. That morning in Tampa I wrote these lessons down with minutes to spare, went downstairs to a packed auditorium, and, with crib sheet in hand, delivered a talk from my heart that I would repeat hundreds of times throughout the years. So much for relying on canned speeches. This new one opened up my eyes to the real world. And every time I give it, I discover that people really do need a hand.

The story that sparked that life-changing speech became the basis for this book. The pages that follow are a narrative that shares the story of my recovery after my right hand was paralyzed in Rome, and the liberating discovery I made that morning in Tampa: Success is in everyone's hands. It's always there and as simple to use as counting to five. *Thumbs Up* is a simple roadmap that will guide you to a happier life. The steps, and the five chapters of this book, go like this:

1. **Give the world a thumbs up.** Regardless of your situation, when you raise your

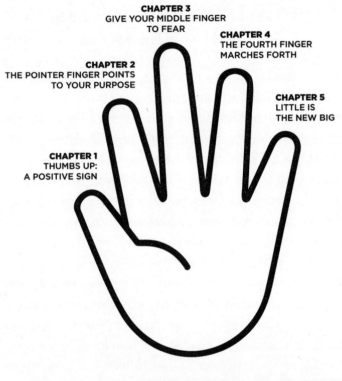

CHAPTER 3
GIVE YOUR MIDDLE FINGER
TO FEAR

CHAPTER 4
THE FOURTH FINGER
MARCHES FORTH

CHAPTER 2
THE POINTER FINGER POINTS
TO YOUR PURPOSE

CHAPTER 5
LITTLE IS
THE NEW BIG

CHAPTER 1
THUMBS UP:
A POSITIVE SIGN

FIVE POINTERS FOR SUCCESS

thumb, you raise your chances of success. Being paralyzed presents one of life's greatest challenges. It certainly did for me when I lost the use of my right hand. But when I gave my prognosis the thumbs up, my hand and my life were up and running within a year. I turned my optimism into a belief system called *optimalism*: the belief that optimism creates optimal outcomes.

2. **Point to your purpose.** Your pointer finger points to your purpose in the world. To say that you have a purpose means you are not here for yourself but for something greater. Mahatma Gandhi's purpose was "to wipe every tear from every eye." Purpose is your *why,* and when you discover your why, you can point at any what, where, and who and make your dreams happen.

3. **Give your middle finger to fear**. Fear is our most misunderstood emotion. Thousands of years ago it saved us from being eaten by tigers by creating a "fight or flight" response. Good news: It's no longer needed today. But all too often that old "watch out" mechanism alerts us to dangers that are less life threatening, like public speaking. As you will learn, giving

fear your middle finger sends fear back
into its eons-old cave.

4. **March forth.** The best way to rid yourself
    of dissatisfaction is to take action. That
    is what our fourth finger calls us to do—
    march forth! Action is the great divide
    between winners and whiners. Action gets
    things done. For thirty years I have closed
    all my businesses on the fourth of March
    so that my employees would make it their
    business to march forth on their dreams.
    They use this day off to take the day on.
    What will you do this March 4th? By
    the time you finish this chapter you will
    know.

5. **Little is the new big.** Your fifth finger is
    a reminder that the little things in life
    bring us the biggest joys. I call them
    peak moments—small in time but giant
    in spirit. A little thank you, a little hug,
    a little prayer, a little help, a little walk,
    a little time, a little thought make the
    biggest contributions to a world that has
    become a little crazy.

The biggest untapped resource in the world is
your purpose. I ought to know. I wrote my last book,
*The Story of Purpose: The Path to Creating a Brighter
Brand, a Greater Company, and a Lasting Legacy*, on
how companies' brands and leaders with purpose in

hand could reach new heights never imagined. Now I am sharing an even more important story—yours.

A life of purpose begins in the palm of your hand. For thousands of years, fortune-tellers looked at peoples' palms and foretold their future. Called palmistry, this art was popular probably because what you heard became a self-fulfilling prophecy.

Today, superstition aside, what you tell yourself is what you sell yourself. That's why Thumbs Up works—because your purpose is all about your unique gifts and talents. To find your best self, you need to start with your best Thumbs Up thought. A life of purpose begins to build when you give yourself the thumbs up. The rest will follow.

This book is not about the pursuit of happiness. It's about the *result* of happiness that comes from giving yourself the GO sign.

The word "inspire" is from the Latin *inspirare,* which means to breathe in. In a world that is out of breath, this story is an invitation to the Age of Inspiration, a time when we will look to the greatest resource humankind has—the human spirit.

With the right mind-set, everything is in reach. Even peace. Imagine for a moment a world in which people smiled upon one another, pointing to greater community, putting fear aside, and marching forth hand in hand, all doing just one little thing for another. Ultimately, our human attitude will determine humanity's altitude.

Success in business, as in life, comes in many shapes. How do you grab it today and make it yours?

This handbook will teach you how to use your hands to pick up more than you ever dreamed was possible. Deeper love, more meaningful work, better health, greater wealth, and richer faith are all within your grasp.

It begins with giving yourself a hand. Now take my hand and let's begin the journey.

CHAPTER 1

THUMBS UP: A POSITIVE SIGN

Thumbs Up people are positive people. The energy they create attracts all the goodness the world has to offer. Thumbs Up people wake up every day feeling excited and go to sleep every night feeling safe.

Thumb through the pages of history and you will discover something remarkable. The first thumbs up was not an accident. When early primates' opposable thumbs first touched their index finger, it allowed them to grasp things. One of the most important things we would come to grasp was the idea that the future was in our hands.

There is no simpler way to say "Way to go" or "Good job" or "I did it" than raising your thumb. It's a universal gesture for "I've landed on the moon" or "I've landed on my feet." It's a signal that says "Watch this." It's a symbol of courage and encouragement, an acknowledgment that I believe in me and I believe in you. It's a way to give yourself or someone else a hand.

A thumbs up is an affirmation to the world, a stranger, a friend, a teacher, a parent, a child, or a significant other. A thumbs up is a prediction that what you are about to do will succeed. It's a hooray, a flag raised, a wave of assurance, a stamp of approval, an icon, a badge of optimism, a "like" on Facebook, a salute to victory, a wink to what you love. A nod to God.

Giving a thumbs up is not just good body language. It's a hug from your heart. It's proof of your intention in the present and your faith in the future.

No other finger operates quite like it. Even though it's the shortest finger, it has more power than any other and more muscles dedicated to its reach.

WE ARE BORN LOOKING UP

It should come as no surprise that when you raise your thumb, you raise your chances for success, wellness, and love, increasing the possibility of achieving the life you always dreamed of.

A Thumbs Up attitude begins with a sign and a thought. It starts with the all-important awareness that you can change your thoughts and change your life. If you are constantly seeking reasons to be positive, you are more likely to influence what you think. The ripple continues, and other ripples will follow.

Roman emperors called their thumb signal *pollice verso* and used it in the notorious Coliseum. Thumbs down meant a quick death for the gladiator. Thumbs up indicated that he should be spared. Though the days of gladiatorial combat are long over, the thumbs up sign still signifies life some twenty-three centuries later!

We are all born looking up. Then we strive to stand up and grow up. But along the way we encounter people and events that can lower our gaze and bring us down. We all need a hand. And that's why I wrote this book.

Thumbs Up is not a handbook about how to avoid being down but a story about looking up in the face of adversity. Bad things happen to all of us. It's how we respond to those challenging moments that defines us and determines the course of our lives.

By paying attention to even the most seemingly insignificant thought, we can rewire our life's path. It begins by raising your thumb.

Think about it. When you consider doing something positive, you have a choice to act on that intention or not. When you decide to share a positive thought, it's because you gave yourself permission to do so. The same goes for talking yourself out of a positive thought.

So, think about whom you've been listening to. How's that working for you?

Zap a negative thought and try reacting with a Thumbs Up response. Notice what's right. Share the love. Show your appreciation and gratitude. The goal is to nurture and give life and attention to productive thoughts. It's about banishing the negative, blaming, finger-pointing thoughts that underestimate the power of good.

How we react to the little moments in our lives makes the difference between the happy and hapless, the helpful and helpless, the hopeful and hopeless.

GIVING THE THUMBS UP
SIGN ISN'T ALWAYS EASY

Sometimes just getting your thumb up feels nearly impossible. I know firsthand. Facing one of the darkest hours of my life, I learned that when you give a thumbs up, the world looks up.

After partying in Rome one evening in 1975 with an actual princess, I was a passenger in a sports car that broadsided a bus at fifty miles per hour. My right arm was crushed in the accident, leaving my hand paralyzed.

The timing could not have been worse. I had journeyed all the way to the Cinecittà Film Studios to intern with the great film director, Federico Fellini, and had not even started work. Worse yet, I was twenty-two years old and felt that my life was over. Who would love me without a hand? Who would offer me a job? Mind you, this was the pre-Paralympics, pre-wheelchair-accessible era.

The ambulance race to a nearby hospital was a blur, but the Italian word *amputazione* quickly focused my attention. The hospital reached my mother, who flew to Rome to find me in post-op. The doctors had saved my arm but not its ability to move. They said that with lots of physical therapy there was a slim chance I might be able to raise my thumb.

I never forgot that. To the doctors it was a medical prognosis. But to me it became an anthem for life— raise that thumb and the rest will follow.

Choreographing hundreds of bones, muscles, and nerves in my hand was difficult enough, but keeping a positive attitude was the real hurdle. I couldn't just assume that it would happen. I had to take charge and keep in mind a positive image of my hand moving. When the negative thoughts started to creep in, I would chase them away. I *had* to see my hand moving. I *had* to believe that image could beat paralysis. I *had* to say to myself, "I can move my thumb. I can do this."

GIVING ANOTHER A HAND

My mother arrived with a gift in hand. It was a Saint Jude medal that she purchased in Rome a few days after her arrival. Saint Jude is the patron saint of lost causes. Mom figured it would work for me. She attached it to a gold watch fob and placed the magical necklace around my neck.

Santo Spirito, the hospital where I'd been taken, was the oldest and most holy of hospitals in Rome. The nurses were nuns, crosses adorned every wall, and century-old frescos told stories of healing. This was obviously a place where miracles could happen.

I remember believing that the medal was a sign that some greater force would intervene. Perhaps Saint Jude Thaddeus? *Thaddeus* is a Greek name that means "great-hearted one." Catholics celebrate him as the Saint of the Impossible. He must have been an eternal optimist as well. He had to be if he was going to cure all of these incurables, including me.

The next day, after my mother arrived, I was visited by a South African minister who was quite sure I could get the use of my hand back by believing so (which I took to be another sign). He quoted Mahatma Gandhi, who said that if you have an idea and take action on it, that action becomes a habit. That habit changes your character and that new character determines your destiny.

GIVING MYSELF A HAND

The idea on which I took action was getting my hand back in working condition. The minister said that feat was up to me. If it's to be, it's up to me. A simple concept. Say it out loud. *If it's to be, it's up to me.* Now think of an idea that is dear to you. Have you taken action on it? If so, congratulations. If not, this book is a good first step. As I learned, the work begins with you and your beliefs. What we think about is what happens.

I had two choices: hand my destiny over or take it over. In a defining moment, I made a choice to not give up on what seemed impossible. I found and surrounded myself with positive forces—nuns, patients, doctors, visitors, my mother, and Saint Jude, all of whom believed that I could get that thumb up.

We are given two hands to remind us that one hand needs another—whether it's the hand of a friend, a parent, a priest, or even God. As John Lennon quoted Yoko Ono in his final interview, "A dream you dream alone is only a dream. A dream you dream together is reality."

By taking action in soliciting their support, positive thinking became easier for me and felt more like habit. I shifted my mind-set from the hand I did not have to reaching for my dream to write.

WRITE YOUR OWN SCRIPT

Just as the minister had predicted, my new habit of optimism changed my disposition, perspective, spirit, and, yes, character. I felt stronger, as a person of character does. And that character is who I would be for the rest my life.

During my convalescence, I realized that if I could become the author of my own script, I could write my next chapter. I was determined to define myself rather than be defined by others.

Life is full of authority figures—people who give you orders, make decisions for you, and try to control you with rules. Well, here is something to always remember: The word "author" is in the word "authority." When you author your story, you become the greatest authority in your life.

THE DAY I LIFTED THE WORLD

The day I lifted my thumb was the most uplifting day of my life. And from that moment on, I have held the power of positive thinking close to me and have never let it go. I had won. My thumb moved because I believed it would and I made it happen. And just like the doctors said, my other fingers would follow its lead. That's the power of being Thumbs Up.

No gesture is more positive than a thumb pointing straight to the sky. Soldiers do it before going into battle. Astronauts do it before blasting off into space. Rock stars like the Beatles give it to their fans. And I would raise my thumb thousands of times after Rome, 1975.

I did it after my wife Cynthia and I exchanged vows and said farewell to our wedding party twenty-four years ago. I did it for my sons, Alden and Julien, when they came up to bat at little league games and when they went off to college. Did it when I sold my company, did it again when I bought it back. Today, I do it before going into business meetings and after I win the business.

Thinking Thumbs Up is the core of resilience. *Being* Thumbs Up means you are open to opportunities.

How many times have you given a thumbs up? To your spouse at the beginning of the day? To your child after a great recital? Everyone has given the thumbs up sign. The trick, of course, is to do it every day and look for the possibilities to be positive.

If our thumbs spent less time down on our iPhones and Androids and more time up in the air, we would realize the real joys and possibilities of life.

GROWING UP THUMBS UP

My mother was a formidable influence on my Thumbs Up development. She lavished me with attention and infused me with confidence and an unswerving belief that I could do anything. As early as I can remember, she said, "Joey, you can do it. Joey, you're the best. Joey, you're a winner." She constantly played the song "The Impossible Dream" from the Broadway musical *Man of La Mancha* and was telling me to *just do it* long before Nike adopted the slogan.

I've read that when your parents are your biggest fans, you're bound to go on to bigger audiences. Picasso's mother told him, "Pablo, if you can become a soldier, you'll be a general. If you become a monk, you'll end up a pope." Instead, he became a painter and wound up as Picasso.

Parents need to remember that being supportive means nurturing our children. Giving them confidence in themselves rather than conning them into doing something Mom and Dad want them to do.

For my ninth birthday, I received a present that summed up my mother's belief in her son—a miniature White House. Just big enough for me and a few visiting dignitaries from school. The message? If

I wanted to be president, all I had to do was vote for myself.

WHEN LIFE GIVES YOU A THUMBS DOWN

Life throws us constant curves, and I've certainly seen my share. But the toughest of all came in September 1981 when my father Henry was diagnosed with a rare form of adrenal cancer. I was twenty-nine. He was just sixty-two. We were both too young to get that news.

My father deteriorated in front of my eyes. On December 4, 1981, he lost his battle and I lost my hero. It's been said that it's easier when death is not sudden, but believe me, no matter how long an illness lasts, the end is always sudden. Sometimes beginnings are as well.

After the funeral, my mother said that my dad had left no will, no insurance policy, and no money and that she had no means to support our family. Boom! All of a sudden, I had a family to support. We were broke and broken-hearted. I still remember looking inside my wallet at a twenty-dollar bill, wondering how my $30,000-a-year salary from advertising could support all three of us and pay the bills. I might have just enough in the bank to pay for my dad's funeral.

My younger brother Michael and my ailing mother were scared. I was, too, but this is where resilience comes to the rescue.

A week after burying Dad, I had to take action. I took charge and did everything I humanly could do to help my mom and my brother, and the rest is history. No one ever said life would be easy. And boy, it was not. It took hard work, a united family, learning how to ask for help, and giving more than receiving. It's amazing how much we learn about ourselves when tough times hit.

Resilience is part of everyone's DNA. Even during the darkest days for my family, something inside me said, "Joey, get creative and get going." That's the way I define resilience—your best idea plus action. You might say I had no choice, but we all have choices. I chose life.

My father's passing left us out in the cold. Michael, who was closer to my father than I was, was deeply bereaved and my mother was in a state of, well, shock. She had been married to Dad for thirty-three years.

Those lessons in the Italian hospital came careening back. Time to pass the Thumbs Up forward. It was time to give a thumbs up and somehow get my brother and mother to do the same.

BEING THUMBS UP WHEN LIFE KNOCKS YOU DOWN

Life can be cruel, but I have learned that even when bad things happen, the outcome is based on our outlook. Take Roger Ebert, the most famous film critic in the world. Co-host with Gene Siskel of the popular TV show *At the Movies*, he was the only film critic ever to win a Pulitzer Prize.

In 2006, his voice and ability to eat and drink were stolen from him when cancer forced the removal of his jaw. Ironically, his horrific situation led to the most prolific time of his life. Through his loves, losses, and struggle with alcohol, Ebert maintained a "two thumbs up" appreciation for life and love.

Ebert believed that when you are doing something you love, fear gets pushed to the back of your mind. As Ebert succinctly says in *Life Itself,* a biographical documentary about his legacy as one of the most influential cultural voices in America, "Make your heart your face."

In his memoir of the same name Ebert wrote, "I believe that if, at the end of it all, according to our abilities, we have done something to make others a little happier, and something to make ourselves a little happier, that is about the best we can do. To make others less happy is a crime. To make ourselves unhappy is where all crime starts."

The omission of making yourself and others happy is an unlawful act. Break the law enough and you go to jail. Then you feel isolation, a separateness that keeps people apart. Kindness, on the other hand, is a good deed that creates unity, not selfdom. It's the ultimate "get out of jail free" card.

WHEN THINGS GET OUT OF HAND

One of the most powerful strategies to get life back on track is to create a plan of action. Most people look for immediate solutions, but the irony is that your plan *is* the solution. A plan gives you a path and line of sight. It changes your feeling from falling apart to coming together. So create a plan and thumb through it daily.

There is great power in beginnings. Our first love, our first job, our first house are permanently seared into our memories. Relish your beginnings. We learn and thrive from new hobbies, new friends, and new ways of looking at life. We get many first chances and the opportunity to start over, especially when our plans don't work or it's time to make new ones.

But starting over is also tough. It certainly was for my mom, brother, and me, but we did it. We moved into a small apartment, developed a plan, and pursued it together. We had to reach for larger opportunities in order to deal with the looming challenges, which seemed to grow by the day. In order to make ends meet, we had to focus not on endings but rather on beginnings.

My mother had to focus on life without my father and how to keep his memory and spirit alive. Faced with the harsh lesson that life is not a dress rehearsal, my brother and I had to figure out how to do something we would love that would also be productive.

None of us know when our end will come. But I have learned that in every beginning you'll find a renewed hope, faith, and spark of optimism and possibility. But you must believe it to achieve it.

The best way to take life in is to take life on. And that's what my family did. I had already survived a serious car accident, and it was no accident now that we got hit hard again with my dad's untimely death. This time I knew I had to reach even deeper to remain Thumbs Up, or I'd bring everyone down.

MAKE A LOVING, NOT A LIVING

My mother and brother and I agreed that we would rebuild our lives as a team. My mother would write astrology columns and my brother would embark on his dream to become a pilot. Both pursuits had been dormant, but now they had the impetus to pursue them. Mom and Michael had held themselves back from being their fully alive selves. Now it was time to take action.

I already loved being a copywriter on Madison Avenue. The 1980s were even more fun than the 1960s were depicted on the wildly popular TV series *Mad Men*. It was more like *Glad Men*.

Being raised with a Thumbs Up attitude and having to literally get my thumb back up helped me enormously. Being positive has a generative effect. Try it! The point here is with an all-thumbs-in attitude, we were able to make not just a living, but a *loving*.

As my mother, the astrologer, reached for the stars and my brother's aviation career took off, I was climbing the ladder of success. At age twenty-nine—less than a year after I'd lost my father—I became the youngest executive vice president of a global advertising firm.

How did I do it? By loving what I was doing. Taking the risk to ask for a meeting with the CEO of the company and requesting my salary be doubled. The CEO was my hero. He knew I respected his work and he made sure I knew he valued mine. I was working on purpose. My purpose. Doing what I was supposed to do.

When you love what you do, it doesn't matter where you end up. You are already a success. It's the Law of UP—if you are not looking down at the world, you will move up.

And I was looking at the top job in my field—chief creative officer of the New York office—when I got a call I wasn't expecting.

It was from the chairman who said I would not get the job. I was too green. Really? Instead, he offered me the top creative spot in an outpost called Atlanta, Georgia. I was crestfallen. It felt like a thumbs down. But was it?

I arrived at D'Arcy MacManus Masius Worldwide in Atlanta in February 1984. Within two years the agency tripled in size, winning pitch after pitch and landing me on the cover of the national publication *Ad Age.* I had stuck my thumb up and out, hoping my success would get me a ride back to New York City and the Big Job.

But instead I received a call from another thirty-something ad guy. That call would lead to the partnership—Babbit & Reiman Advertising—that would take the industry by storm. Within eighteen months, we were billing nearly $100 million. We won thirty-two out of thirty-five pitches and were known for giving the thumbs up sign with the same gusto that Zorro left his iconic Z.

WHY I LEFT AD-LANTA

Eventually our agency became famous, but my passion for advertising was waning. I sorely realized the world was ad rich and idea poor.

After I'd been punching the clock for almost twenty years, the clock was punching me back. My father's deathbed counsel came back to me: "It's not the time you spend at the office but with your family that counts."

I share this story for those of you who think your net worth is what makes you happy. It's not. It's your self-worth that makes you rich, and that can only come from loving yourself, what you do, and, if you're lucky enough, the one who completes you.

I learned that the real ladder of success is the one leaning on your home, and to always put dreams before the dollars. My advertising career was ending so that I could begin living my real purpose.

BUSINESS GIVES A THUMBS UP TO HUMANITY

I closed the doors of my advertising agency in 1994 and opened the world's first ideation company, BrightHouse—a consultancy whose purpose was to make the world a brighter place.

For too long business was in business for itself, giving anything that did not make itself wealthier the thumbs down. I decided it was time for business to give society the thumbs up by making more good more available to more people.

That year, BrightHouse was tapped to help bring the Paralympic Games to Atlanta. Paralympic players come from all walks of life, though many can no longer walk. Or see. Or use their hands. But they all think Thumbs Up, which takes them to breathtaking athletic and personal heights. The disabled are superabled because they have overcome. They teach us that though we can't correct the wind, we can adjust the sails.

The tagline I wrote for the Games that year was *What's Your Excuse?*, followed by the sentence *The Olympics is where heroes are made, the Paralympics is where heroes come.*

This was my first taste of what advertising could do if it added a "D"—ADDvertising, which means creating ideas that would add to the world. Unknown to me at the time, BrightHouse was starting a movement for businesses to become positive and purpose-focused.

THUMBS UP: THE MOVEMENT

Thumbs Up is not just a book or a sign; it's a movement and the way forward.

A thumbs up is a boomerang that comes right back to you. It returns with a smile, good feelings, a better day, good karma.

This book is your permission to start a ripple of Thumbs Up all over the world. If more people like you looked up, perhaps the world wouldn't be quite so down. When we uplift others, we uplift ourselves. So give a thumbs up daily. It works. Send a signal to society. This is your mission as a passenger on this planet: a vision for a world without fallen gladiators and a purpose big enough for all.

From this day on, help people go forth by giving them a thumbs up. Get in the habit of sharing praise. Even one thumbs up a day counts. Watch what happens. I guarantee you will get one in return. A smiling hand can reach higher and grab more of life and love.

When you give your kids, your spouse, your employees, or your clients a thumbs up, you are validating another life, person, action, or deed. A thumbs up is a universal sign of healing, happiness, joy, approval, validation, and purpose. It is the silent expression that speaks the loudest. One thumbs up can change a life. Start with yours.

TWO RULES OF THUMB

As you read this book, keep in mind that it's time to celebrate life with a simple gesture that has a big message. Remember my two rules of thumb; both are easy to execute but require practice:

1. Give yourself the thumbs up.

2. Give negative thinking the thumbs down.

If you can raise your thumb, you can elevate your life. Your mind can only hold one thought at a time, so why not make it a positive one?

For me, a thumbs up was a positive sign and the beginning of my comeback after being told I might never move my fingers again. Lying in that hospital room, I thought the worst—that I would lose the use of my hand. Without a hand, no one would love me and no company would hire me. I would be alone and die.

I uttered the word "should" thousands of times. I *should* have gone to law school. I *should* have gone to the opera instead of the disco. I *should* have gotten her phone number instead of getting into the car. We all "should" on ourselves incessantly.

Shoulda-coulda-woulda thinking is the roadblock to every destination in life. Instead, we need green-light thinking, which is a mind-set that says *go*. But what do you do when your bones and nerves are broken? You create a breakthrough.

There is a Native American story about a very young warrior who goes to his grandfather, the chief of his tribe, with a conundrum. "I have two wolves inside me," he tells the chief. "One wolf is hopeful, spirited, and kind, and the other wolf is mean, competitive, and evil.

"Who will win?" he asks.

The grandfather pats the young warrior on his head and says, "The one who will win is the one you feed."

During my darkest hours, I had found life's secret: You are what you think.

FROM THUMBS UP TO LOOKING UP!

Living Thumbs Up is not just a mind-set. It's a reset. This new way of thinking changes the way we take on life. Because when you *feel up*, you love to *show up*; you are more likely to *follow up* and definitely *speak up*. When you *look up* you see your highest self.

Think of it as your secret formula. Like the Coca-Cola Company, whose secret formula is said to refresh the world's spirit, you, too, have a secret for renewing your spirit and making life sparkle. Focus on looking up and I promise things *will* look up.

What's more, people who look up don't look down on others. They don't try to "one up" each other. So much unhappiness stems from comparing ourselves to others.

Happy, joyful, content people move up because they show up, follow up, speak up, look up, and avoid staying stuck in their own circumstances or those created by people who give them a thumbs down.

Thumbs Up people view others' needs as a cause greater than their own. When we are Thumbs Up, we stop thinking only about ourselves. When that happens, it's amazing who enters our lives and what happens when they do.

Thumbs Up people are both problem solvers and solution seekers. They act on their dreams and ask for help. There are no back burners. Thumbs Uppers live a life free of regret or dreams delayed. They never put life on hold.

Here are some inside secrets to staying Thumbs Up—and on the up and up. Each chapter helps you use your own "hand" book, starting with your thumb. When you raise your thumb, you raise your hand to life. Creating a Thumbs Up attitude will help you adopt a whole new altitude.

LET'S START THINKING UP!

1. **Think up**. My mother always said, "Thoughts have wings." Remember, your attitude creates your altitude. This book is about setting the stage for thinking your way to a better life—at home and at work.

2. **Show up.** Woody Allen said, "Half of success is showing up." Without showing up, you are not present. Your presence is key. Avoid being invisible. That's called *presenteeism*—your body is present but your mind is elsewhere.

3. **Follow up.** With my first book I got a resounding "NO" from publisher after publisher until one finally said yes. Walt Disney went to 302 banks before one gave him a loan for what the others considered a Mickey Mouse idea. Don't stop until it's a go.

4. **Speak up.** "Tell them about the dream, Martin," yelled gospel singer Mahalia Jackson the day of the March on Washington. Deviating from his script, Martin Luther King Jr. spoke up. His "I Have a Dream" speech awakened our nation's hopes and buried our hates.

5. **Look up.** Life is looking up in more ways than one. First, life is looking up to the stars. That's where we are from. Yes, we are made of stars. It is also looking up to something Greater. We are hardwired to seek greater meaning. And when we do, we say to ourselves, *"Life is looking up."*

Many believe we are the amalgam of what happens around us. But I believe we are the product of what happens inside our heads. As I had learned at the Italian hospital, we are what we think. So don't say, "I'll believe it when I see it." Say, "I'll see it when I believe it." Say "no" to no and "yes" to yes. Say yes every day to something new that you know could add meaning and purpose to your day and to your life.

At the hospital, I thought yes. *I can do it.* That is how I got my thumb to move and, in turn, moved my world from hapless to happy, from helpless to helpful, and from hopeless to hopeful.

We now know that thumbs-down thinking suppresses the immune system, raises blood pressure, and creates stress and fatigue in the body. We also know that a positive attitude creates positive chemistry in your body and between bodies.

It's your choice.

In his bestselling 1946 book, *Man's Search for Meaning*, Viktor Frankl, a Holocaust survivor and psychotherapist, wrote, "The last of the human freedoms—to choose one's attitude in any given set of circumstances, to choose one's own way."

This sentiment, from one who witnessed the worst horrors known to humanity, is further testament to the Talmud quote in the beginning of this book: "We do not see things as they are. We see things as we are."

Freedom is the state of free will. That will rests in our minds and, when awakened, that will can stop every "won't" in the world.

THE THUMBS UP RESPONSE

Sometimes it's hard to keep your thumb up. I know. We have all survived challenging days, often blind-sided by problems or difficult choices, stuck and unsure of what to do next. One thing is certain: Problems do not go away, but your way of handling them makes all the difference in the world.

Miracles from upstairs happen every day. But miracle workers on the ground create many more through the actions they take. This is what I call your "response-ability"—how you respond to life's down-turns and turndowns.

Downturns are when plans don't go as planned. Thumbs Uppers don't shut down or shut up. They have another plan, their backup plan. Having plan B is the best way to succeed when plan A does not work.

In my early days of advertising, my boss never let me go to a client with just one winning campaign; I had to bring two that I loved. Then the decision would be between options one and two, not winning or losing.

Turndowns are when you feel rejected. A love interest, a client, a job interview, or a school turns you down. Again, Thumbs Uppers believe that the rejection has little to do with them. They know it's not their issue but rather due to reasons beyond their control. And if it is their issue, they see the moment as a learning opportunity to get it right the next time.

GIVE TODAY A THUMBS UP

Now is the most important time of the day, because this is the time when everything in your life can change. For Thumbs Up people, "some day" is not a day of the week. Dwelling on the past has no future. Today is a GIFT, not TGIF.

Ask yourself this question: What will you do today to make your dream happen?

Do you believe it is possible to turn *impossible* into *I'm possible*? Then do something right now.

There is a wonderful and true story about survivors of a plane that went down over the Amazon jungle. The survivors were sure they would be found so they stayed put. Soon food and water started to run out. On the tenth day, they were beginning to lose hope when one survivor found his. "If they can't find us, we need to find them," he said. And off he went. He soon discovered rescuers and managed to save his crew.

Now, when he gives speeches about the incident, this scrappy survivor ends his talks with one question: "When is your tenth day?"

Thumbs Up people don't put off; they take on. Giving yourself a thumbs up can kick-start your life right now.

GIVE ONE THUMBS UP A DAY

Getting my thumb up in that Italian hospital room was a miracle. I remember my first thumbs up to the doctors. Getting one back confirmed I was coming back.

We all have thumbs-down days and challenging events in life. We're pulled down by loss, grief, disappointment, failure, illness, and the list goes on. Pain is inevitable, but experts have concluded that most of our suffering is optional.

Some days are darker and tougher than others. Life presents tragedies that the human spirit can't wrap its mind or arms around. Yes, everyone is coming back from something. Sometimes you lose something or someone or just lose your way. That's why a Thumbs Up thought or attitude or even a glimpse of hope is so comforting. It's a signpost that says you are on the right track. And even if the road is long, the journey back to hope and happiness is possible.

Speaking of tracks, imagine you are a hitchhiker. You put out your thumb for a ride. Someone stops, opens the car door, and invites you in. This stranger helps you get as close to your destination as possible.

It works the same way in life. When you stick your thumb out, your chin up, and offer someone a hand, people stop, open doors, and invite you into their lives, all of which helps you—and them—reach your dreams. With this in your heart, give one person a thumbs up today. You will witness the power of praise. When you give yourself or other people a thumbs up, you are sending a message that they are important. Being a source of positivity is a gift you give yourself and the world.

Raising your thumb raises all ships. Use it in mentorship, show it in friendship, and give one to your relationship. It improves workmanship, scholarship, and leadership. The only ship it sinks is hardship.

I give everyone I meet a thumbs up upon parting because that is what I want to impart—to leave them with an unequivocal confirmation that they are headed in the right direction.

OPTING IN FOR A LIFE OF OPTIMISM

Opting in to the life you have always dreamed of requires giving yourself permission. It takes adjusting. We have to think a different way. Instead of seeing insurmountable obstacles in our way, we have to see our way around them.

If you are physically safe, there is nothing stopping you from going on the path to your dreams. Try it. Set your mind on your dream. That's called a mind-set. Then become adaptable. This is the hard part, but if you adapt, no setback can stop your positive mind-set. This is the secret. Adaptability overcomes what might otherwise be overwhelming. Adaptability is the power to adjust to your circumstances. This is called optimism.

When you believe that things will turn around, they do, not because they change but because you changed your perspective. It's how America survived the Great Depression, world wars, and environmental disasters. We saw our way around them and in doing so we saw a better way ahead.

By remaining optimistic, we can focus on making our dreams happen. This adaptability leads to an unrestrained future and profound joy.

Optimism awakens our deepest human drive: to never give up. In this way we see the opportunity, not the obstacle, and push forward to our dreams. Remember, adjusting your mind-set to Thumbs Up resets the mind to look up, since it's not what happens that is important, but our attitude toward each happening.

Former prime minister of India, Indira Gandhi, said, "You can't shake hands with a clenched fist." The opposite is true as well. Clench your fist for a fight. Now raise your thumb. Your fist just made a friend and peace is at hand.

CREATE HAPPINESS WHEREVER YOU GO, NOT WHENEVER YOU GO

When I was a kid, I would watch my grandmother perform a little trick that made other people instantly happy. She would spread the fingers of one hand and place a cloth napkin over that hand. She would pull one corner of the cloth down through her thumb and index finger and then tightly close those digits. Then she would pull another corner of the cloth through her index finger and middle finger and close them as well. Then she would tug on the cloth in the same two places to make napkin "ears." Presto—a regular napkin was transformed into a rabbit with a nose, ears, and a nibbling mouth.

Now, fifty years later when I see a child or adult who needs cheering up, I find a restaurant napkin, and make "Oma"—the bunny I named after my beloved grandmother. I follow Oma's formula and watch the magic work.

Wherever you spread cheer, you create magic.

This was my Oma's way to give the world a thumbs up. It was a simple trick and her way to share a smile wherever she went.

FROM ROAD RAGE TO ROAD SAGE

Years ago, I was in a traffic jam in Atlanta. It was late in the day and frustrated drivers were honking their horns. I remember a car that cut me off and pulled ahead. I got caught up in the moment and became irate. I pulled up to the car with the intent of giving the driver the middle finger, but in the moment I decided to give him a thumbs up sign signaling all was okay. He was surprised, to say the least. He rolled down his window, returned the thumbs up, and said, "Have a great day."

I never forgot that moment, and to this day I take every chance to give fellow drivers the right of way with a thumbs up. Imagine if we all gave each other a thumbs up when we were in a jam, traffic or otherwise.

OPTIMISM HAS A GOOD RING TO IT

"I am the greatest. I said that even before I knew I was," boasted heavyweight champion Muhammad Ali.

In the boxing ring of life there are two kinds of people: those who want the bell to ring to end the match, and those who do not. When you are slugging it out and winning in life you feel the rapture of being alive. Sure, we all take the punches and the jabs, but what matters is that we swing back.

Former US President Theodore Roosevelt said, "Far better it is to dare mighty things, to win glorious triumphs, even though checkered by failure, than to take rank with those poor spirits who neither enjoy much nor suffer much, because they live in the gray twilight that knows not victory nor defeat."

Here is a man who did not want the bell to ring. Wanting the bell to ring is not always a bad thing, though. Like a boxer who is hurt and needs a breather, the ring of that bell is a welcome relief.

Go into round 1 with a knockout attitude, not waiting to be saved by the bell. What saves us is knowing we will prevail, keeping our thumbs up, and knowing the world is in our corner. It is interesting to note that a boxing glove has two parts. One part protects the four fingers while the other part is dedicated to protecting the all-important thumb.

WAKE UP ONE DAY AT A TIME

Let's explore this idea of waking up. Today let's wake the soul, an essential part of the spirit. Wake up your actions. The art and act of waking up your thumb to reach upward as I did after my accident is the first step. This chapter sets the stage for making your life more peaceful and meaningful. Without a Thumbs Up attitude, it's hard to get past your own problems.

Start small but think big. You don't have to take on the world today. But you can take on one day, one hour at a time, starting with the moment you wake up. Wow! Imagine that every day you WAKE UP in more ways than one.

Your first breath of the day is hugely important. What idea are you inhaling? I hope it is, with awe and wonder, *I am alive*. Wake up and make small, significant changes to your life and they will add up.

I wake up on the right side of the bed. Here are some of the ways that make my day better and keep me feeling awake, alive, and alert—Thumbs Up even on down days. Keeping a few Thumbs Up rules at the top of my mind helps me better listen to myself.

Top Ten Thumbs Up Tips

1. **Wake up Thumbs Up.** Your first breath determines the breath—and breadth—of your day. Take a minute to imagine what you want to accomplish today before jumping out of bed. Remind yourself what's right with your life. Envision a positive, helpful day, in which you reach out to others. Count your blessings even if you can only get to one.

2. **Turn off the noise.** The words "silent" and "listen" have the same letters. Find a quiet place and listen to your heart, not just your mind, today. Meditation often works better than medication.

3. **Be extra nice to everyone until 10 A.M.** Try it. I have found if I am pleasant through midmorning the rest of the day takes care of itself.

4. **Under-schedule yourself**. Make all one-hour meetings fifty minutes instead. This way you will have ten minutes to decompress, readjust, and take on the next meeting fresh.

5. **Think for a living.** At my company, BrightHouse, we are paid for our ideas. So we spend four hours a day in thought.

Give your thoughts some thought. Invest in yourself: "I think, therefore I am valuable."

6. **Walk the walk**. Learn something new. Then, take a walk or imagine yourself walking around a park and think about what you learned. Your insight will have time to set and register.

7. **Wonder? Leads to wonder!** Ask more questions. When it comes to exquisite thinking, questions are the answer. Try this exercise. The next time a problem comes up, ask "Why?" five times. Each time you ask, you will get closer to the truth. Here's one to start: Why are you reading this book? Okay, you take the next four.

8. **Be a *whys* guy**. If you know your *why*—your personal purpose or what you love to do—you will make better *what*s. Purpose is where your unique gifts and the needs of the world intersect. So, why are you here?

9. **Reward daydreaming.** When Albert Einstein was asked what a typical day at Princeton University was like, he replied that 20 percent of the time he taught students and 80 percent of the day he

stared out the window. Dreams are much better when you are awake. So put time aside every day to dream. A mind at play produces more and better ideas than a mind at work. As Einstein said, "Creativity is intelligence having fun."

10. **Call it a day**. If we could really end our business day at 5 P.M. we all would live another ten years. Enough work, it's time to love—your mate, your pets, yourself. After all, everything else in life is a consolation prize for love. And keep in mind that tomorrow is another day to be Thumbs Up.

TAP INTO YOUR WELL-BEING

As this chapter comes to a close, my challenge to you is to stay Thumbs Up even when life wants to drag you down. Think about what gives you joy and do it.

A story comes to mind that might help you during those trying moments.

When our son Julien was six he was feeling down. He'd had a bad day at school and was really sad. I told him about the *well-being*—a story about how every human being has a well inside him, and if you reach down into your well, into your spirit, you'll find your well-being. It is a beautiful well, and if you go deep enough you'll find a wonderful stream of fresh, clear thinking that will refresh you, restore you, and renew you.

At first Julien seemed confused. "How could a well live inside us?" he asked. He looked at me and said, "Daddy, do you have a well-being?"

I said, "Yes, and you are a big part of it." He smiled and seemed to understand.

Tapping into your well-being creates more of, well, *your* being. It's quite simple. It is only when we reach down that we can we touch our heights. Try it. Reach deep into your well of dreams and hopes and you will discover a wellspring of vital energy.

Coming back after my accident, my ability to find a way forward for my family after losing my dad and to discover lightness after the darkness of depression are proof that the *well* in our *being* never goes dry.

When you bounce back, life becomes a ball. And when you have the ball, you have it all. So get those thumbs up and watch what happens when you point yourself in the right direction.

If this book is about one thing, it's about understanding your *why*—what you were born to do, meant to be—and taking action toward that *why*. Taking action on something is important, but knowing where you're headed is what we'll discover in chapter two.

FINGER TIPS

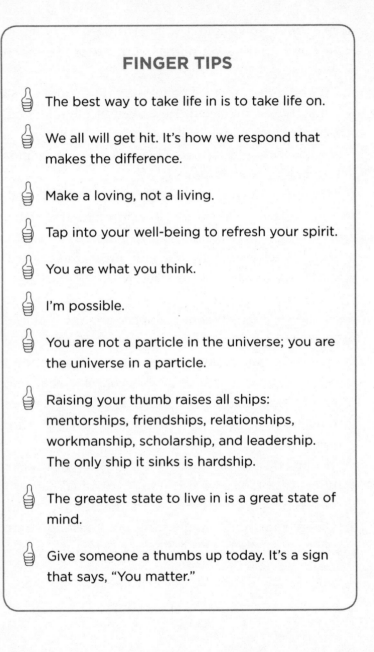

The best way to take life in is to take life on.

We all will get hit. It's how we respond that makes the difference.

Make a loving, not a living.

Tap into your well-being to refresh your spirit.

You are what you think.

I'm possible.

You are not a particle in the universe; you are the universe in a particle.

Raising your thumb raises all ships: mentorships, friendships, relationships, workmanship, scholarship, and leadership. The only ship it sinks is hardship.

The greatest state to live in is a great state of mind.

Give someone a thumbs up today. It's a sign that says, "You matter."

CHAPTER 2

THE POINTER FINGER POINTS TO YOUR PURPOSE

Using your pointer finger allows you to harness all your positive energy and aim it at your personal goals. Your journey becomes shorter as you keep your eyes on the long-term goal—free from distraction, focused sharply on your target.

With some feeling coming back in my second finger came a feeling of immense joy. Movement in two fingers helped me shift from the memory of a nightmarish car crash to thinking more positively than ever about my dreams for the future.

Now when an obstacle presents itself in my life, I'm reminded that the darkest hours can still enlighten us and help us carry on. I love the story about the monk carrying a lantern into the darkness. The deeper he goes and the darker it gets, the brighter the lantern shines. When something difficult happens, look for the lesson.

For me, the lesson came in a get-well card from one of my nurses at the hospital. It quoted the thirteenth-century Persian poet Rumi, who has inspired and guided me ever since: "Be a lamp, a ladder, or a lifeboat." The South African minister who visited me was the lamp. Those taking care of me were ladders, and my faith in God was my lifeboat.

As many of you do during tough times, I had prayed to God. I promised to do something positive with my hand if God returned its use to me. Little did I know, the IOU would be this book and the discovery of a life built on purpose.

Rome was not an end. It was a grand beginning. And today is yours.

Beginnings have great power. Your first kiss, your first love, your first car, your first day on the job, your first house. Your first step on your journey to purpose.

WHAT'S THE POINT?

The point of your life is to make your point. The index finger literally means "pointing finger" from the same Latin word, *index*. And that's how we're going to use it—to discover your purpose in life.

Some use this finger to scold, as in finger wagging. Simultaneously, we send a message that it's not nice to point. Actually, I believe that pointing is a good thing. Your pointer finger clicks your mouse to take you places. Held up vertically, a pointer finger means first place.

The pointer finger is also called the trigger finger—in my view because when you get your purpose right, it triggers almost everything. When you point at something with your heart, you are creating the coordinates for your destiny. Your purpose leaves a fingerprint on the world.

DEFINING PURPOSE

The word "purpose" finds its origin in the Old French word *porposer,* meaning to put forth, and the Old French word *porpos*, which means intention.

For some Native Americans in the Pacific Northwest, purpose was written on their totem poles dating back to the early 1700s; for sailors it's the beacon of light that guides them back to safe harbor. The Jedi call it the Force, and others call it a calling, your reason for being, your essence, your *why*, your DNA. I define purpose as what defines you. What you do with that purpose is what redefines the world. Purpose, then, is the reason you are living.

In this chapter we will excavate your purpose. I say excavate because purpose comes from within. It calls from your heart, and when you answer that call, you truly begin to live.

THE CALL TO ADVENTURE

We are all called. The question is, will you answer or hang up? My call came in 1975. It took courage, but I boarded the *SS Leonardo da Vinci* for Genoa. As my parents waved goodbye I gave them a thumbs up and set out for my destination—Cinecittà Studios in Rome to work beside Federico Fellini, the legendary filmmaker of *8½*, *La Dolce Vita,* and *Amarcord*. The boat was leaving two weeks before my graduation, but when the ship's horn bellowed, it was my commencement. My adventure was in motion.

Thousands of miles and years earlier in Harlem, a young lady also got her call, starting her own adventure. She was only seventeen years old when she was invited to the Apollo Theatre to dance before a sold-out crowd. Poised and polished from years of instruction and performance, the young woman said a prayer and stepped onto the stage.

But instead of dancing, she sang a song that shocked the crowd and changed the musical world forever. When this young lady recognized her true talent in life, she was living her purpose. It wasn't what she had originally signed up to do. But the legendary Ella Fitzgerald knew she *had* to do it. Have the courage to take your call.

THE FIRE WITHIN

Each of us is born with an instructive spark of fire. When fanned, it warms our souls; when ignited, it lights our path. It is the torch of your authentic self, and it has the power to brighten the world.

Your purpose is your timeless truth. There will be only one of you through all time. Ignore this and the fire goes out. Heed it and you will burn brightly on earth.

PURPOSE BEGINS IN
THE BEGINNING

I believe purpose was created with the Big Bang. This instantaneous expansion of the universe had two characteristics, intention and contribution—the same qualities as purpose. Scientists tell us that the universe is still expanding. That's intention. And like purpose, the Big Bang made contributions beyond itself, namely the stars, the planets, and all of us.

If my theory is correct, then along with its sister, gravity, purpose is a force unto itself. But unlike gravity, which pulls downward, purpose pushes forward.

Put it all together and each of us is a mini-universe moving forward with intention in order to make a contribution beyond ourselves.

JUST BETWEEN YOU
AND THE WORLD

The Greek philosopher and scientist Aristotle believed that your purpose is found at the intersection of your unique talents and the needs of the world. What a great place to start the journey to find your role.

Here's an exercise to help you along: Draw two intersecting circles. Write down your talents in the left circle, and in the right circle write what you believe are the needs of the world.

At the intersection is the sweet spot where you serve yourself *and* others. Here your life gives life.

Here your passion turns its eye to compassion and the one-of-a-kind being called "you" calls for more kindness in the world. You still need to make a living, but here you discover that "meaning" is what really makes a life.

Don't worry about getting the words right. It's much more important that you be on the right path—one with heart. At the end of the chapter we will return to this exercise.

THE BEST STORY

Human beings are meaning seekers. That's why we love stories.

When we were kids a good bedtime story put us to sleep. As adults a good daytime story wakes us up.

Your life tells a story. It's a movie in the making. You are the director, the producer, the writer, and the costar—the other star is your North Star. In your universe, this star guides and inspires you to be your brightest self. In this way, you can brighten others, because you don't belong to only you. The world needs you.

Keeping a Thumbs Up mind-set helps you focus on a target the way an archer aims for the bull's-eye, a pitcher seeks the strike zone, and a golfer zones in on that tiny cup.

PURPOSE IS TENACIOUS

While writing this book, I met a wonderful couple who have two daughters with diabetes. These purpose-driven parents wanted to create a drink that their daughters and other teens could enjoy without the caffeine and sugar.

They came to me with their story, and I loved it so much I partnered with their company, Tenacious Tea. They wanted some marketing advice and I told them that the best people and brands all have great stories. Tenacious Tea is no different.

They already had an amazing story. They *were* tenacious, even with a mountain of obstacles before them. Sometimes we pick the mountain and other times it picks us. We all face this metaphorical mountain in our lives and we have a choice—scale it or fail it. Be tenacious and we will reach unimagined heights.

Tenacious Tea proves that where there is a will there is a way, successfully flying off of grocery store shelves. And the way is straight up!

THE BIGGEST QUESTION YOU WILL EVER ASK YOURSELF

For many years, I have been teaching business students at Emory University the power of purpose. Though the curriculum prepares them to bring greater purpose into the business world, it also inspires them to bring their own personal purpose to the world at large.

I explain that they can choose among many paths, but only one is truly meant for them. Everyone has a unique gift. To never discover it would be sad, but to deprive the world of it would be tragic.

What if Jonas Salk had gone into real estate? What if Thomas Edison had been a banker? What if Gandhi's life mission had been to be a professional wrestler? What if Einstein had aspired to be a singer— or if Ella Fitzgerald hadn't? What if Susan B. Anthony had become a mountain climber? The world would be a very different place.

The biggest question you will ever ask yourself is this: *What future benefit might the world never receive if I do not discover and contribute the talent that is uniquely mine?*

- Will the cures for cancer and Alzheimer's go undiscovered?

- Will a new company that employs thousands of people never be founded?

- Will a technology that could end global warming go unfinanced?

- Will a future nuclear conflict fail to be averted?

I end the class with this challenge: Discover where your talents and gifts intersect with the needs of the world.

Be honest with yourself. Discover your purpose. Then point it at the world.

SUCCESS OR SUCK-CESS?

Sometimes I think the word "success" is misspelled. So many people I meet who are considered successful are in a job or career they don't want to be in. That's why it's so important to create your own definition of success.

One thing is for sure: Webster lied. His dictionary defines "success" as "financial gain," yet so many people who are financially successful are flat broke on the inside.

Let me tell you a story about a corporate titan in his late fifties who graced the cover of a major business magazine. In the cover photo, he stands atop a mountain. Clawing at his heels are his admirers—VPs, SVPs, EVPs—who long to touch the hem of his $5,000 suit. The magazine writer crowned this man the king of finance on Wall Street.

The story talked about his path to success, his unflinching focus to create shareholder value, and his planned early retirement that year after he'd worked tirelessly to reach his ultimate achievement.

The man anticipated plenty of time to enjoy his family and the fruits of his labor. After all, that was what he had worked for. Unfortunately, this Master of the Universe never tasted that fruit. He didn't even get to see the magazine cover. His epitaph highlighted his legacy: leaving behind a well-disciplined company.

His misfortune provides numerous lessons. First is that the person who sits on top of the world needs to remember that the earth rotates every twenty-four hours. Second, the road to success ends at your front door. And finally, it's our self-worth, not our net worth, that makes us rich.

My father worked every day of his life except his last. On that day, lying riddled with cancer, he said, "Joey, don't work so much. It's not so important." Have you ever known anyone who in his or her last hours said, "I wish I had spent more time in the office?"

We must not live to work; we must work to live. We have become experts at what we want and novices at what we need. What we truly need is to feel alive. And that happens only when we focus on making a life, not just a living.

Ask yourself if you have the wind behind your back or a whip flogging your backside. If it's the wind, you have purpose. If it's a whip, you don't. No worries, though. Once you discover your purpose, there will be no stopping you. True success does not come and go; it comes and stays.

YOU'RE IN GOOD COMPANY WITH PURPOSE

At the heart of a purposeful company is a leader with a purpose. Take the inspiring leader Akio Morita, for example. In the wake of Japan being leveled by atomic bombs in World War II, Morita cofounded the company we know today as Sony. With only a few hundred dollars in capital, Morita wanted to help rebuild his country. Legend has it that Morita's colleagues presented him a strategy to make Sony the number one technology company in Japan. But Morita changed that strategy to making Japan the number one technology country in the world. Morita dared to dream beyond himself and his company, expanding his orbit of caring to an entire country.

Today, there is a revolution afoot that has companies and brands focusing on greater purpose in service of a healthier and happier world. These organizations are moving from selling goods and services to bringing good and service to the world. In my book *The Story of Purpose: The Path to Creating a Brighter Brand, a Greater Company, and a Lasting Legacy*, I discuss how and why purpose-driven organizations are meaningful and profitable to society and its stakeholders.

Purpose will be the currency of modern commerce. Companies and brands will focus not just on the bottom line but on the front lines—opportunities to create more justice, equality, health, shelter, and global sustainability. Leaders will look beyond next

quarter to the next quarter century. Business will use
the lever of purpose to elevate the world.

PURPOSE IS OUT OF
THIS WORLD

In May 1961, President John F. Kennedy pointed to
the moon. He told his country that by the end of the
decade we would send a man there and bring him
home safely.

Why would the president of the United States talk
about the moon when things on earth were in pretty
bad shape? Issues of racial inequality and poverty
were tearing our nation apart. We were on the brink of
war in Southeast Asia and our economy was teetering.

The reason is purpose. Just like our forefathers
pointed their forefingers westward, heralding our
nation's historic expansion, Kennedy pointed to a
destination that would change our worldview forever.

This act, the president believed, would mobilize
our country with bold purpose. It was indeed a courageous leap as NASA had not even developed the met-
als to build a rocket safe enough for the trip.

It worked. While touring NASA a couple of years
after his announcement, the president approached a
janitor and asked what the gentleman did at NASA.
The janitor responded, "I am helping put a man on
the moon, Mr. President."

Purpose launches more than rockets. It launches
us on a trajectory to the stars.

PURPOSE INVITES US OUTSIDE

Overthinking can drive you crazy. When we think beyond ourselves to help others, we bypass the noise in our minds. When you volunteer or mentor, you leave the confines of your head and enter the arena of the heart.

One winter, I received a call from an Atlanta homeless shelter asking if I would volunteer my advertising agency to join the fight against homelessness via a marketing campaign to raise awareness. I declined, since I was in the midst of pitching a big piece of business. I was working a crazy schedule, getting no sleep, and worrying about the future of my fledgling agency.

On the way home that night, I saw a homeless man sleeping in front of my condo. It was cold. As I entered my toasty home, I thought about the call I had received that day and if this destitute man was a sign from above that I should be helping the homeless. The next morning, I called the shelter back and signed on to help. Even though the pitch was due in a week, I needed to do this.

And if I was going to do it right, I decided I would have to live in the shoes of that man asleep in front of my condo. To feel what it was like to be homeless, I dressed in the shabbiest clothes I could find and staked out a corner in downtown Atlanta. It was another cold night. I asked for money for hours and not one person gave me a dime. Just after midnight, however, a homeless man asked me if I wanted a blanket. I thanked him for the warmth of the blanket and the warmth of his soul. That night I was also given the gift of a new perspective. We are all homeless until someone reaches out a hand to help. And then it hit me. I knew how I could help.

The homeless man's gift of a blanket gave me an idea for an ad. The next day I created a billboard with a big working thermometer on it. Under the temperature it read *Room Temperature for the Homeless.* That night it was 28 degrees in Atlanta.

The billboard went up the day of the pitch, which went well. A week later, the client called to tell me we had won the business. I thanked him and asked what put us over the top. Creative strategy, research? "Actually, it was the story you told us about the night you slept on the corner downtown."

I continue to volunteer. It clears the head, opens the heart, and feels so good that you almost feel selfish to benefit so richly.

THE PURPOSE OF CUTTING THE ROAST

When searching for your purpose, authenticity is important. It has to be your gift, not one passed down or prescribed to you. Purpose that is made up doesn't make out.

Once, a little girl was watching her mother prepare a pot roast dinner. Her mother told her that the first thing she must do to make the best pot roast is to cut the end of the roast off before putting it in the pan.

When the little girl asked why, the mother said, "Well, that was the way my mother always did it. Let's call your grandmother and ask her why."

The grandmother replied, "Well, that is how my mom always did it." The young girl then asked to visit her great-grandmother to find the answer.

After some cookies and tea, the little girl approached the family matriarch and asked, "Great-grandma, why do you cut the end off a roast before you cook it?" Looking across the three generations with a quizzical expression and a smile in her eyes, the matriarch replied, "Because I never had a big enough pot."

How many of us are making pot roast Mom's way or working in jobs or living in a relationship that our parents think are perfect? If you are, you're living out their fantasies—not yours. This is not the recipe for success.

THE PURPOSE OF SECURITY GUARDS

Remember your first love? Everyone has one. Remember your first breakup? Everyone has one of those, too. Mine happened when I was fifteen.

We had been seeing each other for most of eighth grade. But when the summer rolled around, she told me that she was in love with another boy, a ninth grader who played basketball. This was very important to her.

I was not a sports fanatic. I thought Shea Stadium was a French restaurant. And now a jock would win her over?! I was crushed.

I went home and decided my best move was to get some flowers, write a love letter, and go to her apartment building. In order to get through the lobby I had to sign in with the security guard. His name was Thomas. He immediately recognized me and rang her apartment. After a moment he hung up the phone and said, "She says she's busy." I left the letter and flowers with Thomas, who said he would send them up.

Crestfallen, I went home and told my parents, who were not very empathetic and assured me I would get over it. That did little to console me. I thought the world was coming to an end. I went over to her building every day that week. Thomas would ring her apartment and the response was always the same.

On the fifth day Thomas said, "I don't think she wants to see you. Why don't you have a seat?" For the next hour we talked. Thomas shared a story about the first girl who broke up with him. *Gee,* I thought, *his story is worse than mine.* Suddenly, I did not feel quite so devastated. He told me to come back and talk anytime. And I did.

For the next two weeks, Thomas and I talked about girls, school, and life. The last day I saw him was the day before his vacation. He said, "Joey, I want to show you something." He pulled out a picture of a woman. "Do you know who this is? This is my bride of forty-four years. She is also that first girlfriend I told you about. If you are meant to be," he said, "it will be."

Thomas gave me hope. In his own kind and tender way, the security guard offered me the security of knowing that things would be okay.

Who is your security guard? Are you aware of the insecurities that you are guarding? For whom are you serving as a security guard? To be one you just need a badge of empathy and to know that it is better to be interested than interesting.

DISCOVERING YOUR SKY MAIDEN

Although the actress Gwyneth Paltrow got some criticism for using the term "conscious uncoupling" to describe her divorce, I'll borrow from her playbook and call purposeful love "conscious coupling."

I am certainly not a marriage counselor or expert on love, but after twenty-four years of matrimony and seeing many of our friends split up, my wife and I can tell you that agreeing on the shared purpose of your marriage goes a long way to making it work. For many of our friends, the words "just married" have a different meaning after the excitement wears off. It's more like they are "just" married, as in "no more than that." In fact, there is *a lot* more to what makes a successful marriage.

In his book *Who Needs God*, Harold Kushner recalls a tale that delivers a secret for lasting love:

The members of a certain West African
tribe tell the legend of the Sky Maiden. It
happened once that the people of the tribe
noticed their cows were giving less milk
than they used to. They could not understand why. One young man volunteered
to stay up all night to see what might be
happening. After several hours of waiting
in the darkness, hiding in a bush, he saw
something extraordinary. A young woman
of astonishing beauty rode a moonbeam
down from heaven to earth, carrying a
large pail. She milked the cows, filled her
pail, and climbed back up the moonbeam
to the sky. The man could not believe what
he had seen. The next night, he set a trap
near where the cows were kept, and when
the maiden came down to milk the cows,
he sprang the trap and caught her. "Who
are you?" he demanded.

She explained that she was a Sky
Maiden, a member of a tribe that lived in
the sky and had no food of their own. It
was her job to come to earth at night and
find food. She pleaded with him to let her
out of the net and she would do anything
he asked. The man said he would release
her only if she agreed to marry him. "I will
marry you," she said, "but first you must
let me go home for three days to prepare

myself. Then I will return and be your wife." He agreed.

Three days later she returned, carrying a large box. "I will be your wife and make you very happy," she told him, "but you must promise me never to look inside this box."

For several weeks they were very happy together. Then one day, while his wife was out, the man was overcome with curiosity and opened the box. There was nothing in it. When the woman came back, she saw her husband looking strangely at her and said, "You looked in the box, didn't you? I can't live with you anymore."

"Why?" the man asked. "What's so terrible about my peeking into an empty box?"

"I'm not leaving you because you opened the box. I thought you probably would. I'm leaving you because you said it was empty. It wasn't empty; it was full of sky. It contained the light and the air and the smells of my home in the sky. When I went home for the last time, I filled that box with everything that was most precious to me to remind me of where I came from. How can I be your wife if what is most precious to me is emptiness to you?"

And so the Sky Maiden was gone forever. This tale reveals that the secret to love goes beyond looking into each other's eyes. It's seeing the world *through* the others' eyes, sharing not only your bed but the dreams that you have in there. When you meet your Sky Maiden, make sure that you are not just falling in love with his or her looks. Instead, keep in mind these three looks: (1) look into each other's eyes, (2) look into each other's hearts, and (3) look at one another and share what you see.

When each of you sees the other's dream, you will find your path to the stars.

THE PURPOSE OF BOOKS

The purpose of books is to find ourselves in the story. The word "read," from the Germanic origin, actually means "to advise to put in order." That is the purpose of the Magic Library, the name I gave our library at home.

It started as a way to encourage my sons' love of reading. Later, the Magic Library became a place to hone their imaginations. Every time they had a question and were stumped, I would say, "Let's go to the Magic Library and ask a book for the answer."

We would walk into the library, and my sons would close their eyes, put out their pointer finger, walk to the chosen book, open it, and read one sentence. They would find in that sentence a clue to the answer.

One time we were trying to decide what to have for dinner. Julien, six at the time, suggested we ask the

Magic Library. He selected the book *The Courage to Be* by philosopher Paul Tillich, and the sentence he read aloud was, "Joy is the emotional expression of courageous."

Julien deducted that if we eat more courage, we would have more joy. We decided on pizza with mushrooms since Julien thought eating a mushroom for the first time would be very brave.

Over the years, the Magic Library has offered up endless insights and answers for everyone in our family. The library has taught us the power of imagination. The books in there are like little time machines that take us from our home to places throughout time—from *wonder?* with a question mark to *wonder!* with an exclamation point. Most wonderfully, they have helped us write our own stories.

Once I asked the library where I should take the family on vacation. I closed my eyes, stuck out my forefinger, and followed it to the book spine of *The Godfather* by Mario Puzo. The next day, we booked tickets to Sicily, where Francis Ford Coppola filmed much of the movie adaptation. The library made our family an offer none of us could refuse.

PURPOSE IS THE HANDIWORK OF THE SPIRIT

Connect with your purpose and you will connect with those who have gone before you, for purpose is at the heart of everything. It is the spark that creates the fire in your soul. That flame not only kindles your spirit but brings warmth to others.

When you put a thimble on your forefinger, you use it for mending something that's torn. Hardship can tear into lives, but the common thread that runs through humanity is a purpose greater than ourselves.

Purpose is the handiwork of the spirit. Purpose heals what is hurt and gives life to us when we feel lost. Everyone you meet today has lost something or someone. The purpose you choose has the capacity to help them find newness and aliveness.

THE PURPOSE OF LIFE

Too many of us are living the dreams of others. Our culture, our education, even our parents can steal our real purpose in life. Then there are those loving souls that release the dream within us.

Recently I heard about a conversation between a mother in hospice and her daughter, who had spent her life trying to meet her mother's expectations. The daughter adored and respected her mother, so much so that she was living her life to make her mom happy. Knowing that time was running out, the mother summoned her daughter to share one last piece of advice.

"Darling, I feel like I have been living inside another woman's body all my life," she hinted. The mother regretted dictating to her daughter the life that she believed was best for her. Her last wish was to free her daughter.

It worked: The conversation sparked a revelation in the daughter. She, too, had long felt the she was living someone else's dream. The next day, she returned to the hospice and shared her elation with her mother: "Mom, I am going to follow that crazy dream of mine."

A mother's work was done.

Being our real selves is really hard. The media paints pictures that blur reality. Billions of dollars are spent every year to tell you who you should be, what you should wear, and how you should smell. It's not good enough to be you. The truth is enough *is* enough.

The poet E. E. Cummings wrote, "To be nobody-but-yourself—in a world which is doing its best, night and day, to make you everybody else—means to fight the hardest battle which any human being can fight; and never stop fighting."

The purpose of your life is to bring your purpose to life—to make your dreams of a lifetime real.

PURPOSE TAKES FLIGHT

I had just taken a seat on a Delta Airlines flight to one of my favorite spots in the world, Cabo San Lucas in Los Cabos, Mexico. Cabo is located at the tip of the Baja Peninsula and is, I believe, God's finishing touch on the world. Just before taking off, a man named

Roberto Sanchez-Mejorada approached me and said he uses my book, *The Story of Purpose,* as a guide to business and life. That chance meeting with the chief mission officer of Qualfon would evolve into a dear friendship and an idea that would help his company become a purpose-driven organization.

Qualfon is a call center company headquartered in Mexico. The organization assists businesses with customer service calls. Last year, Qualfon's leadership asked me to speak about a greater purpose for their call centers and the 30,000 people who work there. Are you wondering how a call center can have a greater purpose? The answer is that Qualfon shifted its positioning from being a call center to a place where people discovered their callings.

Qualfon wanted to help every associate in the call center find his or her own mission in life. Working closely with the leadership team, I guided them in developing a plan for putting their purpose into action: Qualfon would be able to help their employees by educating them about the many opportunities for fulfillment in the world, and then celebrating those staff members who followed their dreams. This way, the associates would be happier and would be more likely to pay forward their joy, even when dealing with grumpy customers.

I love that the company is a faith-based organization, and since the original meaning of the word "religion," from the Latin word *religare,* is to reconnect, Qualfon employees have found that the connection is between their heart and their head. Purpose is the path from the heart to the head.

YOUR STORY OF PURPOSE

For the past two decades, I have helped hundreds of organizations discover their purpose in service of creating a brighter world. That journey is shared in my last book, *The Story of Purpose*. In *Thumbs Up*, I am going to help you find your story of purpose. Let's begin.

HOW TO FIND YOUR PURPOSE IN A WEEK

In a week's time or less you can make a change that will help you have the life you were meant to have, not the one someone told you to have. You will be living on purpose. Everything and everyone else will follow.

Four I's See Better Than Two

My consultancy, BrightHouse, developed a framework called the Four I's (4I's), a process for discovering and articulating an organization's purpose. The Four I's refer to four phases: investigation, incubation, illumination, and illustration. Each phase is meant to bring an organization closer to its core purpose. The process works equally well for individuals.

The Four I's journey will take approximately twelve hours, so you should be able to articulate your purpose in a week's time. Every day, spend some time on one of the 4I's. In a week, I believe you can emerge with the gift called *you*.

Phase 1: Investigation

On day one we journey back to your first days. I like to say, "The fruits are in your roots." By going back to the beginning of your life and rediscovering what you valued and what you loved, you will take your first step on the path of purpose.

BrightHouse starts with an organization's archivist to learn about the organization's beginnings. In your case, talk to relatives about the dreams you had as a child.

Your Assignment: Talk to five important people who knew you when you were a child. Then think about the three most important moments during your education. Finally, imagine that you have $25 million and could not fail at the job of your dreams. What would that job be?

Write it down.

If it doesn't give you goose bumps, try writing it again. And again.

The Result: Your calling (and goose bumps).

Phase 2: Incubation

This phase involves thinking deeply about the world at large, where your talents and the needs of the world intersect lies your calling. What calls you? How will your gifts lead the world to a better place? If Phase 1 was about you, Phase 2 is about you plus the world. At BrightHouse, we call in luminaries—subject matter experts who help our thinkers think about how a business can improve public life with the unique talents the organization offers.

You, too, have luminaries—friends and associates who help expand your thinking.

Your Assignment: Now that you have your calling, write down what most troubles you about the world and how you might bring light to the situation through your work. There are plenty of problems in the world, but they are no match for a person with purpose.

The Result: You find yourself at the intersection of your unique gifts and the needs of the world. You are ready to articulate your Master Idea.

Two days have passed and you have worked on your purpose for about eight hours. The next step is to walk away and let your thoughts marinate. I have found that my best thinking happens when I leave it alone for a while and take a walk. Try doing the same. Ironically, the office is the least stimulating place for thinking, so think outside that box we call the office. The car, the gym, a place of worship, and my shower are my favorite places for "Eureka!" moments.

Phase 3: Illumination

When you've given yourself enough time away and you're ready to revisit the 4I's, it is time to write your purpose. The following checklist will help you discover and articulate your purpose. Then, we will go back to the diagram where you listed your gifts and the needs of the world and fill in that middle circle.

1. **Your Purpose Begins in the Beginning:** Like the oak that sprouts from an acorn, great people grow from seeds planted in their childhood. Go to your baby book or ask a relative to find or share the words that described you in your earliest years. *Write them down.*

2. **Your Purpose Rings True:** Your purpose is a truth about you. While facts about you may change over time, truth never does. What is the one truth about you that needs no proof? *Write it down.*

3. **Your Purpose Teaches:** What was the most revealing thing you ever learned about yourself? How would you share this insight with the world? Give it lots of thought. What do you want to teach the world? *Write it down.*

4. **Your Purpose Makes You Come to Life:** Your purpose is a passion and creates

aliveness. What makes you come alive? *Write it down.*

5. **Your Purpose Is a Battle Cry:** What is your shout-out to the world? What would a T-shirt say if it were all about your philosophy? *Write it down.*

YOUR PURPOSE TELLS YOUR STORY

Food for thought: Salvation Army cofounder William Booth did not have time to send a holiday greeting to his offices throughout the world. As the leader of a frugal organization, Booth searched for the shortest message he could send by telegraph. He used a one-word battle cry to inspire his associates with a lesson that has been telling people who join why they have been here for more than 100 years. That lesson launched an army: The Salvation Army. The word? "Others."

What one word describes your purpose?

MY PURPOSE IS . . .

Okay, it's time to return to Aristotle's two-circle diagram and have another go at articulating your purpose. What is the gift you want to share with the world? Put that gift in the left circle.

Now think about the needs of the world—the world at large and the world at small. Keep in mind, the needs of the world could be halfway around it or in your community or your own backyard. What is the need that you feel needs *you*? Write that need in the right circle.

Carefully review the left side of the diagram, then the right. Now at the intersection, write your purpose— one that captures your gift and how you will use that gift to leave the world a kinder, happier place.

Phase 4: Illustration

The final phase of the one-week purpose journey is illustrating your purpose—literally bringing it to life. This is where you turn your words into deeds. Purpose without action is useless. Today and every day, take one action that demonstrates your purpose to the world.

Your purpose is your timeless truth. Use your purpose and become one of Rumi's ideals. Remember those? As a *lamp,* how will you shine the way for another? As a *ladder,* how will you help someone climb his or her mountain? As a *lifeboat,* how will you save someone's spirit from drowning?

Though the 4I's exercise is my preferred method for finding purpose, there are other ways to discover yours. The important thing is to do it. Whether it takes twelve hours of working the 4I's plan or a different method to discover your purpose, use this as a launch pad to keep yourself on track and meet your goals.

HOW TO FIND YOUR PURPOSE IN A DAY

Say you don't have a week to find your purpose. Try this exercise on a weekend. Connect the dots of happiness. Draw ten circles and fill each one with a time you felt the most joy in your life. When you connect all of those moments you will begin to see the bigger picture—your purpose. If this excites you, and I know it will, try going on the weeklong journey to find your true self.

Your purpose is your motivation, a word that means "an inner social stimulus for an action," stemming from the French word *motiver*. We need a cause bigger than ourselves to feel the true largeness of life.

Purpose puts us in touch with something beyond ourselves, and that in turn connects us to the rest of the world. Serving someone or something else beyond yourself breaks you out of the separation that closes us in and closes everything else off. This is what I love most of all about helping people discover their purpose. You will discover how big, beautiful, and bountiful the world can be if you just let it in.

HOW TO FIND YOUR PURPOSE IN AN HOUR

Okay, you want a quick and fun exercise but don't have a day to find your purpose? Here is how I have helped my friends find theirs in an hour.

Look yourself up in the dictionary. That's right, grab a dictionary and take thirty minutes or so to circle ten words that best describe you. Then write those words down on a card and put it near your driver's license. Why your driver's license? Because these are the directions to your destiny, and you'll need your license to drive there.

I tried this exercise just before opening my consultancy, BrightHouse. I loved the words I found so much that I put them not only near my driver's license but on my business card as well. Here are nine of them: husband, father, author, soul man, thinker, professor, revolutionary, speaker, and jump-roper. I was looking for a tenth to describe how I feel about my family. I couldn't find it, so I created my own word: *famillionaire,* meaning someone who measures success by the love of family. This begins with the one you love, then the ones made by your love (your children), and finally, the love of humankind (your friends).

Our associates liked the idea so much that everyone at BrightHouse has business cards with the ten words that describe them best. After all, purpose is about the business of living our best life.

WITH PURPOSE IN HAND

When the thumb and the finger first touched each other, human beings got a grasp of what was possible. The hand became a tool that built tools that would ultimately shape us. Armed with a Thumbs Up attitude and purpose in hand, nothing can stop you but the fear of not getting there.

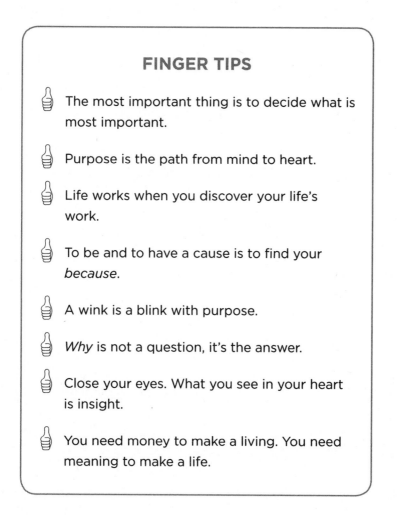

FINGER TIPS

- The most important thing is to decide what is most important.

- Purpose is the path from mind to heart.

- Life works when you discover your life's work.

- To be and to have a cause is to find your *because*.

- A wink is a blink with purpose.

- *Why* is not a question, it's the answer.

- Close your eyes. What you see in your heart is insight.

- You need money to make a living. You need meaning to make a life.

CHAPTER 3

GIVE YOUR MIDDLE FINGER TO FEAR

When you give fear your middle finger, you're telling it to get lost. Only when you lose your fear will you find real happiness. Fear is an illusion and an illness. Reckon with it by leaning into it. This is the only way through it.

G iving someone the bird is an act that dates back to ancient times. It was a gesture that both expressed displeasure and diverted the threat of the evil eye, which is what I had in mind in the hospital when I began to move finger number three. Though my prospects for recovery looked good, I still had my doubts about my future. Will my hand ever be normal? Will I get a job? Will anyone love me if I am disabled?

Fear, the fight-or-flight response that caused us to run for our lives when being chased by tigers 50,000 years ago, remains a force to be reckoned with today. Fear continues to stalk us. It can short-circuit our dreams, leaving us full of doubts, then do-nots, and finally did-nots. Ask yourself these questions:

- How many relationships have you abandoned in your life because of fear?

- How many times have you chosen the safest way because you felt fearful of failure?

- How many career moves have you not made because they were too risky?

- Have you ever feared asking for what you believe you deserve at work?

- What about the fear of doing what you really want to do?

- How many times have you put aside something you were afraid to do?

- What would your world be like if you had the courage to attempt something you fear?

Let's find out.

THE TALLEST FINGER

The middle finger is the tallest because it has the tallest order: to conquer fear in your life and fear's cousins, jealousy and revenge.

When you give fear the finger, you are standing in harm's way. Get fear out of the way and what's left is a clear path to your dreams.

Fear is part of life, but it doesn't have to be a part of yours. By getting to know your fears and rejecting them, they will be a lot less threatening—even losing their power.

When you give fear the finger, you're telling it to get lost so you can find your authentic self. When you abandon your fears, you will begin to feel fully alive, adventurous, and open to new experiences you previously avoided. You will be on your way to the life you have always dreamed about.

FEAR OF THE DARK

I was once afraid of the dark. My parents told me it was due to a housekeeper who used to tell me ghost stories. The fact was that as a child I felt unsafe. My salvation was a nightlight. It kept the monsters hiding away in the closet and helped me quickly find the light switch.

The dark still frightens me. Only now, the dark represents the tunnels we go through in life and the holes we fall into on the way to building our dreams.

Nobody lives without fear, but shining a little light on the darkest part of the night will bring comfort and resolve. In this chapter we'll move together toward the light. Face your fears and understand how fear puts dreams on hold and holds hope hostage.

TEACHING OURSELVES
TO BE SCARED

For years, children have been taught scary messages that adults never thought twice about communicating. Kids of my generation were sure that if we didn't brush our teeth at night, the boogeyman would get us. Some of us were even told that in the happy-sounding nursery rhyme "Ring around the Rosie," everyone falls down and then the plague descends on the town.

A world where London Bridge is falling down and Humpty Dumpty can't be put back together again is really a pretty scary place. What are the messages these rhymes convey? Don't rush it, don't push it, don't touch it, and don't do it or you'll get hurt.

Unfortunately, many of us never outgrow the fears of childhood. Do you know that when babies get scared they clench their fists? A clenched fist cannot receive. When adults clench their fists, we cannot receive what the world holds out to us.

WELCOME YOUR PROBLEMS

We all have problems. As discussed, it is how you look at problems that makes all the difference. A problem is a lesson you didn't necessarily ask for, but when you embrace it and search for and discover a solution or a life lesson, you grow.

The Chinese symbol for "chaos" can also mean "opportunity." Problems solved are opportunities.

Problems are games that need to be won. So welcome them in. Just not for too long.

The word "ruminate" means to think deeply about something. The word sounds like *roommate*. Our thoughts are like our roommates. They bunk in our head and talk to us all the time. Sometimes our roommate will ruminate on some negative aspect of our lives. This kind of chatter can unnerve the best of us. Try switching roommates if yours is disrupting your thoughts and messing with your mind.

THE BEST WAY OUT IS THROUGH

The only way to beat fear is to meet it a little at a time. Find out where your fear lurks and when it cries the loudest and go there. Is it before a speech, an interview, at the beginning of a relationship, or at parties? When we can do the thing we fear, the power shifts and the death of fear is assured.

When I was twelve I went to overnight camp. One day I saw all the "cool kids" signing up for a horseback riding and camping trip. I had never ridden a horse before, but I said, "Why not?" The counselor asked me if I could post and canter. I said, "Sure, but my gallop is a little rusty." *Perfect!* I thought. *No galloping, but the rest will be a cinch.*

I must have been on that horse for less than five minutes when he was spooked by a snake. We took off like a bullet at what felt like a thousand miles per hour. The loose stirrups repeatedly struck my ankles as I tried with all my might to hold onto the horse's neck, screaming at the top of my lungs. This must have deafened the horse because the word "whoa" meant nothing to him. My counselor caught up to me and saved my life and my horse's eardrums.

"Never will I get back on a horse," I said. And I never did.

That is, until my honeymoon. Cynthia wanted a real adventure to kick off our marriage. I said, "Why don't we go on an African safari?" She said it was a great idea—as long as we do it on horseback. *What?* I thought. But I wanted to do something special for her, so I decided to conquer my fear and get back on the horse. I took a month of riding lessons to prepare.

Cynthia and I saddled up and rode nearly 200 miles through Kenya. I never fell off, and I even galloped. Believe me, there's nothing like the freedom of riding through the wind—except for the freedom from fear. Our "Out of Africa" adventure was also a trip *out of fear* for me.

THE FEAR OF FEAR

My friend and psychologist, Professor Art Markman, said something to me while I wrote this book that changed the way I look at life. It is sure to do the same for you. It was about the two ways people approach their days—openly or fearfully.

When we approach life with open arms, we live it to engage our ideals and dreams. This leads to happiness and fulfillment.

But when we live life to avoid an outcome, our best outcome can only be relief. Think about it: Dodging a bullet creates a lot more stress than aiming our energy toward our dreams. Put another way, fear of a result results in fear. An approach in which you have the best in mind is the best approach.

THE BIGGEST LIE EVER TOLD

I do not have a degree in psychology, but I have learned a lot about life over the past six decades. One lesson I learned is that fear is an illusion. It's not real. In fact, fear is the biggest lie ever told. I love this acronym for F.E.A.R.—**F**alse **E**vidence **A**ppearing **R**eal.

When you fear something, you are telling yourself a lie. The evidence in our lives rarely adds up to the fear we experience. The fear is a result of projection—negative outcomes we've conjured in our minds.

We tell ourselves stories about how we are not measuring up, not doing the job, not getting the grade, the promotion, the girl or the guy. These *nots* become *knots* that seem impossible to unravel, but the stories they're based on are fiction.

To write our story truthfully, we need to look through a different lens than the one magnifying our fears. It is the lens of reality.

Consider the work of the American psychologist Albert Ellis and what he called the *ABC Method. A* is the activating event that actually happens. *B* is what you believe to be the truth, and *C* is the consequent feelings you have due to your belief. This method became the basis of cognitive therapy, which helps people process thoughts in healthier ways to cope with depression, anxiety, and other disorders. Ellis believed that by changing the way you think about your fears, you could change your response to them. The combination of the actual event, your belief of what that event was, and the consequential action stemming from your belief, will dictate your action.

SAYING "GOODBYE, FEAR" IS AS EASY AS ABC

Here is an example involving my family. The activating event (A) was a call from a pawnshop telling us that our son Alden had pawned a necklace. Coincidently, Cynthia was missing one.

Our belief (B) was the possibility that Alden took the necklace and pawned it. Was he in some sort of trouble and needed money? Our minds raced toward all kinds of possible scenarios, many of them negative. Our angst meters were redlining (C).

When Alden got home, he told us that he had done a good thing. He had sold a necklace for his friend Igor (the necklace was a gift to Igor from his grandparents) so that Igor could buy his parents an anniversary gift.

See how ABC works? The actual event led to a belief that was false, which led to an anxiety-ridden consequence—fear. There was no evidence other than our mistaken thinking that showed Alden did something wrong. In fact, he had done something beautiful.

A more typical example is a teacher or boss telling you that you could be doing better work. You can choose to think (1) that you are a failure, which will lead to anxiety and worry or (2) that you did the best you could, which might leave you feeling disappointed but confident in your ability to improve—and NOT riddled with fear.

Remember, *we don't see things as they are; we see things as we are.* We need to mind our mind-set. Through the lens of fear the world looks like hell, but through the lens of faith, heaven appears.

PUTTING YOUR FEARS ON THE COUCH

When Cynthia and I got married we sought out a top psychologist, Dr. Arthur Cohen. We were very happy. We didn't need help saving our marriage. Rather, we wanted to savor it. So, we went into counseling to be proactive.

Our sessions were sensational opportunities to discover ourselves and plan the life we had always dreamed about.

The meetings also helped us understand the power of intimacy and the fears that can undermine it. We

learned about Dr. Cohen's Bubble Theory, an amazingly valuable framework for protecting a couple's
intimacy.

Here's how it goes. You and your significant other
live in a bubble. No one can enter that bubble but
you—not your children, not your parents, not your
friends. Your bubble is the safe and sacred place
where the two of you build your love with passion,
intimacy, and constancy. Your extended family lives
in the bubble right outside yours. And your friends
live in the bubble outside their extended families'
bubbles.

The Bubble Theory has two rules:

1. You and your significant other create
    a bubble for your relationship that is
    impermeable. No one can get in but the
    two of you.

2. You are welcome to enter the bubbles
    around your bubble—your children's,
    parents', and friends'. But they can't
    invite themselves into your bubble.

Your bubble protects your intimacy. Cynthia and I
found this especially helpful in creating the intimacy
that we still enjoy today.

Put into practice, the Bubble Theory will help
keep your most intimate relationship bubbling with
love and teach others what it means to be a commit-
ted couple. Unfortunately, you bring your fears with

you everywhere you go, even into the bubble. Getting to know your fears, I have learned, diminishes their power.

When the fears do pop up (and they will!), we use Dr. Cohen's four R's: recognize, reject, replace, and reinforce. First, *recognize* your fear. Call it out. Then *reject* it as unsound and unwarranted. Next, try to *replace* the fear with healthier, more loving thoughts. Last, *reinforce* your new, more nurturing thinking every day.

This is not a quick fix or a magic bullet. But it's a great framework to help you think about intimacy and how fear can scare it off. If you *are* looking for something that will change your life in a day, call in the anti-bummer squad.

THE ANTI-BUMMER SQUAD

I have a friend named Danika who lost her way. She had been in a business partnership that soured and she felt stuck. I called her and said, "Let's have Danika Day."

This was a day created just for her and those she trusted. I asked Danika to bring five people to the table, where we would all focus on creating the life she had always dreamed about. We were her anti-bummer squad, and we were there because we cared.

Caring is having a deep knowledge of someone else so that you may help them grow. To have a deep understanding of another, you must listen deeply. And that's what we did. We learned so much about our friend—everything from her love of making pies to her love of connecting people. Caring for another is not about instilling your ideas but distilling their thoughts in service of them. Care is the great enabler of our time.

Our hope was that we could discover what Danika cared about through our caring, and we did. Her future was present. She would create a social media company connecting her clients to everyone and everything. I named her company Everywhere. And now, because she did the heavy lifting—actually lifting herself out of her rut and building her enterprise—her company *is* everywhere.

And the anti-bummer squad can be everywhere, too. A teacher can turn a C–student into a student who seizes the day. Parents can convey that they are present for their children when things go wrong, not just when things go right. We want our children to be happy. A thumbs up will often get them there, but listening up always will. In a unique way, parents are anti-bummer squads for their children. Have a family meeting. Discuss the worst part of your day as well as the best.

Instead of threatening people with firing, anti-bummer leaders fire people up. They see the word "care" in "career." At work and at home, we all need to replace *Who cares?* with *Who do you care about?*

THE FORGETTERY

I have two places in my head for things that happen to me. If the experience is a good one, it gets stored in my memory. If its not so good, I bring it to my *forgettery.*

Of course, there is no part of the brain with that name. But I use it to describe the place in my mind that shreds everything I don't need—regrets, anger, and other negative thoughts that prevent me from remembering all the good stuff.

Sometimes it helps to take yourself to the forgettery. When we get outside ourselves and expand our orbit of caring to include others, life is grander. Forget about yourself and focus on another. As I tell my sons, if you want to impress someone, let them impress you.

FEAR HATES TRUST

Trust is amazing. It is the glue of every relationship. It makes couples strong and safe and leads them to freedom and intimacy. These two words may sound like strange bedfellows, but they're really not. When you have trust you are free to be yourself. When you are truly your genuine self with another, you have found intimacy. Without trust you are not free to be "me," which gets in the way of the intimate "we."

A marriage vow is a trust. When you and another human being enter into such a contract, you put out a contract on fear. Trust is a bounty hunter of the fears that break the bond between people.

PUT YOUR FEAR IN MY POCKET

I've got a confession: I'm scared to ski. At least I once was. While I was on my first ski trip with Cynthia in Vail, Colorado, a ski instructor taught me the secret of being a great skier. He said, "If you let me put your fear in my pocket, you'll be able to ski down this mountain or any other in the world." I handed over my fear and then I swooshed and whooshed on the slopes all day.

Many years later, as my mother lay dying in a hospital room, ten-year-old Alden told me he was scared about his grandmother dying. I told him to put his fear in my pocket. Soon he was sound asleep.

Darkness looks a lot less scary when someone is with you, whether you're facing a mountain or life itself.

THE SAFE WAY IS A
GROCERY STORE

Fearless people live life fully. Anything else is a compromise. Remember what Theodore Roosevelt said about daring mighty things versus living in the "gray twilight that knows not victory nor defeat"? I tried to write something like that for years.

I was once asked by an advertising journal to sum up my business philosophy and everything I know and want to say into one sentence. My response? *The safe way is a grocery store.*

It says it all for me—take the safe way and instead of being made "Head of the Company," you'll end up with the title "Head of Lettuce." And to those of you who have gotten somewhere and don't want to lose ground, I have a message for you. When you minimize future risks by pulling back the reins, forgetting the boldness that made you what you are today, be careful, because you just might fall off the horse.

If you're not taking a risk at work, you're not doing your job. If you're not taking a risk in your relationship, you're missing out on the gift of intimacy. If you're not taking a risk, you're not taking home the rewards. Life is for the living, not for the "*if*ing."

BEFRIEND A FEAR

It helps enormously to share your fear honestly with a partner or a friend.

A friend of mine was petrified of falling off a mountain or other heights. She didn't like the feeling of losing control and ultimately was diagnosed with a spatial disorder that affected her balance.

She shared the problem with her husband and he was empathetic and asked how he could help.

Together they attacked the fear, bringing in a professional to help. My friend's husband learned how to reassure her, to hold her hand as they approached the edge of a height slowly, without belittling or downplaying her fear.

Her anxiety was very real, but she also learned to trust and lean on her husband more. He reaffirmed her and made her feel safe, not fragile. He encouraged positive self-talk and, over time, she made significant progress.

To their credit, they have traveled to many high places including Schilthorn, a nearly 3,000-meter peak in the Alps, and Mount Masada in Israel. My friend still does not love heights, but she has learned to treasure the views and the experiences. She refused to let fear stop her from enjoying life with her husband, a travel enthusiast and fun-loving daredevil.

STOP FEAR COLD

What's worse than fear that's out of control? Fear in control. Every time I got a sore throat I thought, "Oh my God, I've got throat cancer." Okay, I was a little bit of a hypochondriac, but that was my fear.

I would make all sorts of little deals with God on the side. My favorite was, "God, I hope it's a cold. I really pray it's a cold. Oh, please make it a cold and not cancer."

You know what I was doing? I was making a pact with God to give me a cold. Looking back on those days, I realize that I got more colds than anyone else I knew—all because I made a cold the answer to my prayers.

This is the power of negative thinking and proof that sometimes you are your own worst enemy. The next time you are under the weather or feel like you have been left out in the cold, try comforting yourself with good thoughts. They can stop fear cold.

DON'T "SHOULD" ON YOURSELF

What do you fear? Take a moment to think about it and then write it down. Are you afraid of giving a speech? Too scared to speak up? Are you fearful that you will fail at work? Are you scared to ask someone out?

Here's a little trick I learned many years ago. The next time you tell yourself, "I'm scared," exchange the word "scared" with the word "excited."

Both emotions cause a rush of adrenaline in our bodies, but one leaves you with a *woe* and the other a *wow*. And for heaven's sake, stop saying the word "should." It's a terrible word. No, it's the worst word. Worse than any four-letter word I know.

Here's one "should" I strongly recommend. Go to your backyard, dig a hole about a foot deep, write the word "should" on a piece of paper, and bury it.

A simple device I use to ward off foreboding thoughts is the rubber band exercise, which is effective and inexpensive. Put a rubber band around your wrist. When a negative thought pops up, pull it and let go. The thought is gone in a snap.

BREAKING THE SHACKLES OF FEAR

Losing your fear takes concentration. After all, when was the last time you tried to lose something? Try losing your car keys. It's almost impossible when you *try* to lose them because you're thinking of losing them rather than gaining something else. So, if you want to switch jobs, don't say, "I hate my job," but rather, "I love that other job." Then you'll be spending your time finding what you love rather than losing what you hate.

I know it's hard. Fear is everywhere. News thrives on it and for good reason. "Three people dead!" makes a better headline than "300 million people still alive!" My wife, a former TV news anchor, taught me the newsroom rule, "If it bleeds, it leads."

Advertising sells fear. If you don't drive this car, you won't be going places in life. Use the wrong breath mint and no one will talk to you. Most insidious to me is the subtle message that if you use this product, you will be loved. The other side of the coin is that if you don't buy the product, people will not buy you.

It's as if there is a global conglomerate called Misery Loves Company made up of all the negative people in the world. All you have to do to be hired is be scared.

Be fearful. Be negative. And make someone else feel the same way. Today, there are local branches of MLC springing up all over. If you're a card-carrying member, quit. Now!

Fear is addictive, like cigarettes, alcohol, or drugs. Think about all the negative people and situations in your life. Would it hurt you to let them go? Can you let them go? Or are you like the smoker, the alcoholic, or the drug addict who cannot imagine life without the substance? If it hurts to let go, you are addicted.

In fact, people can get used to anything, even if it's bad for them. A study was conducted with convicts who were incarcerated for more than twenty years. Once released, the majority would commit petty crimes in hopes of returning to their comfort zone— the prison cell. We do this all the time, but in place of cells, we have fears. It's time to break out and break free of the fears that imprison you.

GET RID OF FEAR IN A SNAP

It takes time to make peace with your fears. Here is a helpful exercise that uses your middle finger with a little help from your thumb.

Look at your middle finger and visualize a fear that you have. Say it in your mind and let the words travel from your head, down your neck, across your shoulder, down your arm, and up your middle finger until it's so small it can fit only on the tip. Now, snap your finger. The snap you hear is the sound of your fear exploding. It happens every time your thumb goes up and your middle finger goes down. Repeat this exercise in the morning and night before you go to bed. Thumbs Up, fear down.

FEAR OF LOSING IT ALL

Fear of failure is one of the most common fears. One semester in college, my fears convened in my dorm room. My girlfriend had left me for a dentist, so I felt that nobody loved me. I didn't know whether my screenplay would be recognized, so I couldn't tell if I was worthy of calling myself a writer. I wasn't pursuing my parents' career dream, so I thought I had failed as a son. And I was losing my hair.

I called my mother to share my woes. "Mom, my woman left me. I don't have a job. And I'm losing my hair. Chances are I'm going to end up single, homeless, and hairless!"

Mom responded, "Would that be so bad?" I thought about it and realized it wouldn't be the end of the world. I was living and that was what mattered. My mother said, "If you are not living, you are dying." At that moment, I decided I was going to live.

When I changed my attitude, I changed my altitude. Everything was looking up. First, I stopped comparing myself to the dentist. He gets to stare into mouths for the rest of his life. How much fun could that be? Second, I decided I *was* a writer. I didn't need permission from anyone. As Popeye the Sailor Man says, "I am what I am." Third, I realized that what was *in* my head was far more important than what was *on* my head.

The real irony about losing it all is that only when we let go of it all will we have nothing to lose, including the worry about losing it. So let go of everything, because you can't control anything. No one. No thing. Not even your hair. When everything is gone, you are everything.

FEAR OF HAVING IT ALL

There are those who are afraid of heights and those who get vertigo when reaching for lofty goals. That's because most goals fall short of bringing us true and lasting happiness. Reaching the top of our profession or accumulating all the money in the world is not the grand prize. Not even close.

The having-it-all mentality probably gets its start around the fourth grade when we are *degeniused*. Yes, I believe we are all born geniuses, with the ability to dance, draw, and sing. Then, school makes young adults out of us by taking the children out of us.

The word "education" is from the Latin word *educare*, which means to draw out that which lies within— that is, within the students' hearts. Instead, teachers and parents push stuff into their heads. The result is young adults who have memorized life instead of being mesmerized by it. We graduate from school as excellent sheep.

So it's time to unlearn what "having it all" really means. I propose a new definition for having it all: living the dream.

Goals are ephemeral. They disappear once you reach them, and in their place are other goals. Dreams, on the other hand, never die because they are what make life worth living.

Try this exercise. Sit with your loved ones and make a list of goals. Now take money, fame, and success off the list. What remains is a Gold List, which defines your dreams.

Here is my Gold List, for example:

1. To love and to be loved

2. To help my children never lose the child within

3. To have good health

4. To create a home, a soft place to land

5. To write things that make a difference in people's lives

You are not your money, your house, your car, your job, your career, your jewelry, your clothing, your travel itineraries, or your corner office. If you were to lose your goals, you would be left with gold. All that counts is the stuff you *can't* count.

FEAR OF IMPERFECTION

We invest more money trying to look younger than on healing our bodies from illness. According to the *Huffington Post*, Americans spent more than $10 billion on cosmetic surgery in 2011 alone, altering their faces and bodies, hoping that the repair will replace their despair.

Here's the wrinkle: Lifting our cheeks and chins fails to lift our spirits. Movie idol and leading lady Katharine Hepburn never had cosmetic work in ninety-six years of life. She believed that old age was a privilege.

Hepburn must also have been an "imperfectionist." The healthiest and happiest souls I know are those who believe nobody is perfect. For imperfectionists, perfect is imperfect because it is insatiable and impossible.

Perfectionists are the Joneses next door. You know them. They are the people you are always comparing yourself to. *He makes more money. She's smarter and skinnier. They have better jobs. They have a housekeeper. Their relationship is better. He has it all. She's got it easy. They go out more. They have a pool.*

Perfectionists always come up short. They can never be smart enough, rich enough, or young enough. Imperfectionists, on the other hand, *are* enough. And that means they have it all.

Ninety-nine percent of all the misery we feel daily is due to one thing: comparing ourselves to others.

Believe me, if you don't compare, your life becomes incomparable.

Stop asking the mirror who is the fairest of them all. You are. There is no one like you in the world. If you have doubts, watch the movie *It's a Wonderful Life*. It's a story that proves we are all a part of a bigger story.

Perfect needs a comparison. Nothing compares to you. In the perfect world, imperfect is really perfect.

FEAR IS A FORM OF ATHEISM

You are on a personal road to discovery. The road is well lit, which makes it easy to skip down the path, dance down it, run down it, and go down backward. You're not scared because there's light. But there's a dark part of the road to discovery, too—the scary tunnels where you can't see what lies ahead.

It is here that we must be the strongest because if we stop, so does our journey. Fear is a tunnel. And the only way out of it is through it. If you want to face and fight your fears, this is the perfect place to meet them. Because it is in the darkness that we also meet the superhero Faith. The next time fear knocks on your door, send Faith to answer it. You'll find no one there.

Where faith opens doors, fear shuts them. You could say fear is a form of atheism. The only scary thing about faith is you have to take a leap, knowing that the net will appear below. I promise you it will. Keeping the faith means putting those negative thoughts aside and giving fear the finger.

Fear is a disease. It is the illness of our time. Thoughts have wings, and the negative ones must be clipped, because negative thoughts that fly away always carry back negative messages.

FEAR OF SPEAKING

According to the *Book of Lists,* public speaking is our number one fear. I have given more than a thousand speeches that have reached more than a million people. And I still get the jitters when I walk out on stage.

Here are a few lessons I've learned along the way:

1. Lack of fear leads to a lackluster performance. Without empathy, expectation, and nervous excitement, you can't perform your best.

2. Passion is more important than knowledge. Talk about something you love.

3. Don't read your speech. It's a talk, not a read.

4. Break the ice with a joke. It warms up your audience and calms you down.

5. People love an imperfectionist. So be one.

Finally, remember that rehearsal and preparation will head off anxiety. But if you'd rather die than go up there, talk to your doctor about the beta-blocker Atenolol and, if suitable, take one tablet before your talk. It will keep your heart steady while you knock everyone off their feet.

The secret to a standing ovation is this: Lift people higher than they were when you found them. Open with your heart and close with theirs.

FEAR OF DYING

I wonder what our world would be like if we were taught from day one to give back. That giving was more gratifying than getting. Well, our days would be very different. We wouldn't want to just get to work but rather to give ourselves to work. Getting a promotion would be replaced with promoting another's dream. Getting love would go hand in hand with giving love. We would not be trying to get the most but rather to give the most.

Perhaps, then, when we finally give back the ultimate—our bodies—we would not fear death. Rather than fear the end, we would feel we are giving back to the earth.

WITHOUT FEAR WE CAN MARCH FORTH

I know of a Native American legend in which teenagers are taken up a mountain and told to jump from one peak to another. In one particular tale, a teenager, though at first scared, is encouraged by the chief and taught to have faith in his ancestors who all made the leap across the chasm. The teen jumps and, like those before him, makes it to the other side. In so doing he becomes a warrior.

Life is full of chasms to jump. We hesitate less because we are afraid to fall and more because we are afraid to fail. What would you do if you could not fail? What do you love? Do it. Whom do you love? Tell them. Without fear, all of life is possible.

President Franklin D. Roosevelt told a tired and struggling nation, "The only thing we have to fear is fear itself—nameless, unreasoning, unjustified terror which paralyzes needed efforts to convert retreat into advance."

This is not only the most famous quote about fear but also the secret to beating it. Knowing that fear is not real, will not reason with you, and has absolutely no reason to be in your life, you now can march forth.

FINGER TIPS

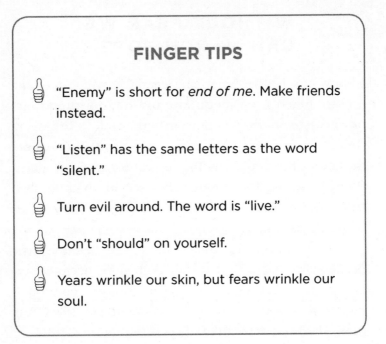

"Enemy" is short for *end of me*. Make friends instead.

"Listen" has the same letters as the word "silent."

Turn evil around. The word is "live."

Don't "should" on yourself.

Years wrinkle our skin, but fears wrinkle our soul.

CHAPTER 4

THE FOURTH FINGER MARCHES FORTH

Only when we march forth can we turn our ideas into realities. Action is the great separator between the Haves and the Have Nots. It turns ideas into I Did It's! Action says, "Don't get even, get movin'."

Vena amoris is Latin for "vein of love," which people once believed traveled from the fourth finger to the heart. While medical science would disprove this, the matrimonial custom of placing the wedding ring on this finger continues. It is fitting, too, that shortly after the ring ceremony, we march down the aisle. Marching forth is an action that turns a vow into a *wow*. And the vow I made in the hospital to get my hand working became a wow the morning when I felt a tickle and a twinge in my fourth finger. My dream was marching forth. Only when we march forth can we turn our ideas into accomplishments. When you move, the world moves with you. Even fireflies know this. They only light up when they move forward.

MARCH FORTH ON MARCH 4TH

For me, March 4th is the holiest day of the year. Every company that I have ever owned closes its doors on that day to celebrate what's most important—marching forth!

Every year on the fourth day of the third month, I encourage everybody to not only take the day off but to take it on—to act, not react. To break free of the superglue that keeps us stuck and be able to move forward in all aspects of our lives.

The best ideas are in graveyards. They are buried with the people who had them but never brought them to life. Winning thoughts that stay in our heads are losers. All of us have a book, a movie, a dream, a Prince Charming, or a great job within arm's reach, but too often we fail to grab it. We all start masterpieces every day. Finishing them is another story. So let our fourth finger remind us to go forth.

START HERE

An action is something we do to accomplish a purpose. Throwing a ball is an action, because you make it happen. Catching one is not, because it happens to you. The same goes for life. It is not happening to you. You make it happen. This is your life. If you want your life to be a ball, you have to put yourself in the game. Getting started is the hard part. The rest is easy. If you don't know how to get started, find someone who did—a historical figure who inspires you.

Try this exercise. If you could have dinner with five famous people from any period in history, who would they be? Okay, so dinner may not be possible, but you *can* read their biographies and learn from their experiences.

Find out who inspired them, what obstacles they faced, and how they got or created their big break. Put them on your personal board of directors so they can help you march forth and build a more satisfying and beautiful life.

Action turns the future into the present. If you want the tomorrow you have been dreaming of, take action today. And remember, if you want something you have never had before, you need to do something you have never done before.

ACT AND YOU SHALL RECEIVE

Thinking by itself will not get you from here to there. Action is the catalyst that turns your dream into something concrete. Power isn't in your bank account or in a Wall Street brokerage house. Power is the collection of actions you take to turn ideas into plans. The literal definition of power is *the ability to act.* Action separates the lovers from the loners, the happy from the hurting, the winners from the whiners. People who take action take all.

Perhaps we should replace the expression "Ask and you shall receive" with *"Act* and you shall receive." History demonstrates that people who have taken action have taken the world by storm. They dream by night and build by day. For them, life is a command. Take it or forsake it.

THE BILL OF RIGHTS

When I give a speech, I often open by offering my audience an opportunity to take a $100 bill from my hand. I hold it up and ask, "Who wants this?" Silence falls across the room, as those in attendance ponder if they should jump up and grab it. Minutes that feel like hours go by as people raise their hands but do not act. I repeat myself once, twice, three times. Inevitably, a brave soul jumps to her feet and runs to the front to grab the money. The audience breaks into resounding applause and regrets not doing the same.

Occasionally, the person who grabs the bill will then offer it back to me, to which I say, "No, it's yours." The others in the audience then kick themselves for not giving themselves permission to take what was right in front of them.

When was the last time you said *yes*? Yes is one of the most powerful words in the universe.

Throughout my speaking career, which spans three decades, people have told me they remember the moment when they weren't the one to grab what they wanted. They didn't put their hands on something right at their fingertips. Imagine what else they didn't grab. Love? Success? Friendship? Opportunity?

It's no surprise that Benjamin Franklin graces the $100 bill, since he is the guy who said, "To succeed, jump as quickly at opportunities as you do at conclusion."

MEET ABE

Abraham Lincoln had the ability to spring back into action after taking fall after fall. That is the power of being resilient. Here is a story that will inspire you to do just that.

Lincoln was twenty-two years old when he said, "I'm going to start my own business." He did it and ended up bankrupt. So he decided to run for the legislature a year later. He lost. So he started another business. It also went under. Fortunately he met and fell in love with an incredible woman during those trying times. "Forget about politics. Forget about business," he said. "I'm going to focus on this beautiful relationship and live on love." During their engagement, she died.

He suffered a nervous breakdown and ended up in an institution at age twenty-seven. That same year he did what anyone who was institutionalized would do—he reentered politics. After years of serving as a member of the Illinois House of Representatives, at age forty-five he ran for Senate and lost the election. A couple years later he ran again and lost again. At forty-nine he ran for the Senate one more time and success again eluded him when he lost the election to Douglas.

Had this tall, determined gentleman not taken one more action, you might never have known his name. At fifty-two years of age, Abraham Lincoln became the president of the United States.

His story is proof of the power of action. Lincoln never stopped marching forth. He was more than a human *being*. He was a human *doing*. And if you're out doing, you'll never be outdone. Lincoln wrote, "Always bear in mind that your own resolution to success is more important than any one thing." When you lose, don't lose the lesson: There is no loss unless you quit.

MEET FRED

Fred Smith was turned down 100 times before someone gave him the money to start a delivery company. Today Federal Express delivers more than a million packages every day. He got there because he absolutely, positively had to be there.

MEET STEPHEN

Stephen Hawking, regarded as the most brilliant theoretical physicist since Einstein, is also an action taker. Professor Hawking has a serious degenerative disease, which has confined him to a wheelchair for much of his adult life. In 1985, he contracted pneumonia and had to have a tracheotomy operation that destroyed his ability to speak.

Communicating with the world would be almost impossible for most people in his condition, but the tenacious professor wrote a best-selling landmark book, *A Brief History of Time*. He teaches in a university today, and his life will teach us forever.

MEET THE GIPPER

When you take action, you take the world into your own hands, giving yourself a vote of confidence. That vote of confidence helped Ronald Reagan turn an acting career into the highest office in the land.

Reagan was given no free rides. He grew up without much money, enrolling in Eureka College to play football. After college, he landed a job as a radio announcer and then became an actor with Warner Brothers Entertainment. Reagan, a natural leader, became president of the Screen Actors Guild.

In 1966, with no prior political experience, Reagan was elected governor of California. Though he lost the Republican nomination for the presidency in 1976, the "Gipper" elected to march forth and run again in 1980, winning both the nomination and the White House.

"Win just one for the Gipper" was a line from Reagan's character George Gipp in the movie *Knute*

Rockne, All American. His most memorable use of the phrase was at the 1988 Republican National Convention when he told Vice President George H. W. Bush, "Go out there and win one for the Gipper."

MEET THE HERO

Hope is how we hold up and hold out no matter what the world throws at us.

I love the story about the gods of Olympus, who gather one day to decide where they should hide the power of hope. Their scheme was to ensure that humans would always look up to them rather than rely on hope.

One god suggests, "Let's hide hope at the bottom of the sea."

"No," balks another. "They will eventually dive down there and find it. Let's bury hope on the peak of the tallest mountain instead."

"No, no, no," answers the first. "They will climb up there before you know it."

After lots of back and forth, the gods finally agree where to hide this awesome power. They will place hope where they believe humans will never look— inside the human heart.

Sorry, Olympic gods. You may be a big deal, but you haven't seen the Paralympic Games. The incredible athletes who participate in this global event have not only found hope—it's their salvation.

In 1994, I was given the assignment to market the Paralympic Games. I learned that these athletes were not disabled but *superabled*. Remember, the tagline I created was, *The Olympics is where heroes are made. The Paralympics is where heroes come.*

This remarkable venue is not about bodies overcoming the impossible. It is about the godlike power of the mind to say, *I am possible.* Paralympians are proof that there are no physical limitations when godlike dreams are at play. Heroes are dealers and ambassadors of hope.

MUHAMMAD, MOSES, AND MORE

Would we have a prayer if Jesus Christ, Buddha, Muhammad, and Moses had not taken action?

If printing had made no impression on Gutenberg?

If Columbus didn't like to travel?

If Galileo went to bed before dark?

If the Wright Brothers never got off the ground?

If Beethoven hadn't practiced the piano?

If Bell had never gotten the call?

If Louis Pasteur hadn't taken a shot?

If Edison had never seen the light?

If Jane Austen wrote only once in a while?

No statue was ever erected to the memory of a person who thought it best to leave well enough alone.

There are two kinds of people who don't like taking action:

1. **Those who live in the past**. They believe that action will cause them to lose something they had before.

2. **Those who live in the future**. They think that taking action will put their future at risk.

I remind both groups that if you keep one foot in the past and one foot in the future, you end up "tinkling" on the present. And the present is where the power is.

So march forth by taking action, now.

ACTION MAKES WORK WORK

What job would make you so happy that you would work for free?

Many of us have jobs too small for our spirits. That's because we put our dreams on hold and hold onto our jobs at any cost. We feel this is something we just have to do but, ultimately, we pay the price. Disease at work eventually can cause disease in the body.

But I believe there's a better way. Let's look at our jobs differently and use the workplace to build ourselves like works of art. Taking action at work means working as the best version of you, so that you can best serve others. That's right, *you* come first. What would it take to be the best version of you at work?

How can you contribute more so that you can grow more and realize your dreams?

One of the best jobs I ever had was as a patient in that Italian hospital. I know that sounds crazy. Though my hand was paralyzed, I learned about optimism, compassion, teamwork, and the power of faith—all the values I hold dear today. Most important, I discovered the power of taking action on what matters most. That includes you.

Remember, being out of work doesn't mean you're out of luck. Broke and unknown at the time, actor Jim Carrey wrote himself a $10 million check, put it in his glove box, and drove around Hollywood going on auditions until he turned broke into a break.

Whether it's an audition, a job interview, or a spot on the tennis team, show up with a thumbs up. If your purpose is great, so, too, will be the result. And the time it takes will not be a factor. Remember, the fastest results come from never-ending patience.

When you can't make ends meet, meet in the middle. It buys you time. By this I mean don't try to fix everything. Rather, make a plan and start working it. If you are overdrawn at the bank, meet with the branch manager and create a payback schedule over time. If your medical tests come back positive, make a plan and take action. Plans help take the pain away by changing your mind-set from "This is coming apart" to "This is coming together."

WHEN THERE IS NO WIND IN YOUR SAILS

My wife's friend worked day and night at his job at the power company, but was not happy or even slightly energized. His passion for sailing, which he indulged on the weekends, was what kept him going. My wife convinced him that if he hooked into his own power to act, he could change his life for the better. He did, and what was once a weekend sail is now a weeklong sailing school where he teaches people how to do what he loves. Adding wind to his sail came from doing what he loved full time.

Not everyone is in a position to open a sailing school, let alone power the wind in their sails. I've been there financially and emotionally. My company has seen hard times, and on a personal level I struggled with a whopping episode of depression that just about did me in. Worse yet, it all happened at once.

In 2004, I broke my foot jumping rope while exercising. The handle slipped out of my hand and I came down on it with my foot. A month later my mother died suddenly, followed by the death of my grandmother. The final blow was that my business was facing bankruptcy.

I went to bed and could not get out. The doctors told me I was clinically depressed. I said that was impossible. I sought help from a color therapy healer, a tarot card reader, a chiropractor, and a yogi. My doctor called me and said, "Joey, you are the Queen of Denial, and I am not talking about the river." He was right. I was denying myself the opportunity to get well.

I spiraled downward to the point that no one around me could help. I was scared to death. At the bottom of my melancholy, I found my only hope. Me. Suddenly, I was no longer scared to live.

SOMETIMES THE WAY TO GIVE A HAND IS TO ASK FOR ONE

Depression is a disease that creates disconnection. Prevention is connection. That's why connecting yourself, or even someone else, with help as fast as you can is critical. Once I admitted I was depressed, I reached out to my doctor for the best psychiatrist in Atlanta. Within hours I was sitting in his office. Within a day he gave me a plan to help me reconnect with the world. Addressing and healing depression takes many caring hands. In them, you can find hope as I did.

During a particularly uncomfortable time, I shared my fears with an Emory University colleague who had successfully battled depression. He asked me to write the following sentence on the front page of a book I was reading: *The key is to remember that this is temporary. You will feel better.* I carried that book everywhere and that message helped carry me. I worked on some little things that made a big difference. Walking and talking are underrated elixirs. Do them together and it can be magic.

Six weeks after my bout with depression, Cynthia and I were talking as we strolled through the mystical gardens of the Self-Realization Center in Los Angeles. Suddenly, I felt that the breeze from the wing of an angel had lifted me back into the light.

My family, physicians, and faith had healed me. When we returned home I got the mail, something I hadn't done in more than a month. I found myself reading a Restoration Hardware catalog, thinking I was being restored. Powerful, indeed.

In the darkness I discovered aloneness. You can't snap out of it or trick yourself into a happier place. There is only one way out. This is the time to break the glass, pull the emergency lever, and call for help. This is not the time to take yourself out of the world. The world needs you. When you are depressed, asking for a hand is not a handout, it's a lifeline. Push together the words "heal thy self" and you get a *healthy self.*

BECOME A FRIEND OF THEIR EXCITEMENT

When we are down, there is nothing better than having a friend to lean on. It works the other way around, too. When we are up, there is nothing better than a friend to share the joy and lift you even higher. And nothing does that better than being a friend of someone's excitement. That means don't squash someone's dream. Instead, give it wings.

On Cynthia's fortieth birthday, we went to an Indigo Girls concert. I had made a sign that read "Sing Happy Birthday to Cynthia" with the hope that the band would lead five thousand people in song. They acknowledged the sign and announced, "We don't have time to sing 'Happy Birthday,' but we are dedicating this concert to Cynthia." The crowd roared with excitement. That's how it feels when one person cheers for what you love.

LIGHTS, CAMERA, AND, OF COURSE, ACTION

Years ago while working at an advertising agency in New York City, I was told that having a window office mean you were really "something." So I found an office with a window and moved in. I never asked anybody. And no one ever questioned me.

An old proverb reads, "When man plans, God laughs." I don't think God is laughing because people are making plans. I think God laughs because people make plans but fail to act.

When I owned my advertising agency, pitching new business was our lifeblood. If you were not winning accounts, you didn't count. So I spent my time not just creating ads but creating experiences that would create new clients. I inundated our prospects with visits, correspondence, calls, and love for what they were all about.

When we pitched a coveted Bahamas business, we covered 40,000 square feet of our office space with sand. For a Trump Casinos pitch, we had all our desks removed and blackjack and roulette tables moved in. For a fast food pitch, I transported the whole team by bus to clear tables at the company's flagship restaurant. For an African American–run airline, my partner and I bought a billboard across from his office window that read, "We Are the Right Brothers."

One of the largest car brands in the world was uneasy about my agency because we had never had an automobile account. When the client walked into our boardroom he saw one of his company's cars on the conference room table. Yep, on the table. We had disassembled it in the lobby and reassembled it thirty floors up to show them that we knew their product inside out.

My agency was one of dozens pitching the Del Taco Mexican restaurant chain account. Ultimately, it came down to two agencies—us and Them. "Them" was a monster agency twenty times our size and real mean. They had it all except one thing—us!

On the day of the pitch at Del Taco's Dallas headquarters, both agencies brought creative work, a media plan, research documents, and a slew of people. But we had one more little surprise.

Our account people had learned that the Del Taco execs would be dining at a Mexican restaurant in Dallas after they reviewed the two pitches. As their food arrived, so did a mariachi band I'd flown in from

Atlanta. Their opening number? "Cielito Lindo," but with the refrain, "Aye, yai, yai, yai, hire Joey Reiman!" The song was a hit. And the account was ours.

People may doubt what you say, but they believe what you do. So we never, ever stopped doing. We won all those accounts and more—thirty-two out of thirty-five pitches in two years—winning hundreds of awards along the way.

LOL: LIVING OUT LOUD

Texting language is the craze. I want to propose a change to the acronym "LOL," which stands for "laughing out loud." I think it should mean "living out loud," because when you live out loud, you express your 1,000-percent, unadulterated, whole self. If that happens you will be laughing out loud throughout your life. Here are some other abbreviations I like:

AM: action moment

PM: peaceful moment

TU: Thumbs Up

2TU: two thumbs up

HAND: have a nice day

TGFG: thank God for God

JUST DID IT

One of the most successful advertising campaigns in the world is the Nike sneakers tagline "Just Do It." This may be the most enlightening message in marketing history. The company never talks about its product. The hero is the athlete who wears the shoes, taking the action the campaign honors.

We don't need sneakers to make the leap to a better job or into a new field. You win by just doing it.

The suffering of Dr. Martin Luther King, Mahatma Gandhi, and Nelson Mandela was relieved by their love for humankind. Bill Gates and Steve Jobs' passion for their work helped them build a digital future from their garages. The Beatles wanted to hold your hand—and they did. Mother Teresa's love of the poor enriched everyone she touched. Even Orville Redenbacher proved that if you love what you do, it isn't corny. Even if its puns that you love.

BECOME AN ACTION HERO

"Look . . . up in the sky!" These words introduced Superman, who first appeared in a comic book in 1938. The words lifted heads toward the sky. Well, it works the same way at work. When your actions protect and help others, you become an action hero colleagues look up to.

Just like Superman, you have the power to transform from a mild-mannered civilian into a super hero.

The Man of Steel acts in his own self-interest; by helping others, he is helping himself fulfill his destiny. What is your destiny? How will you use your strength to lift the world and help your associates march forth?

Action heroes are on a mission. They are not leaving this world until they leave a mark on it. These are their three superpowers:

1. **Super strength:** People who take action have herculean strength. They lift the world up.

2. **The ability to fly:** Joy is the result of helping others. My wife, Cynthia Good, has helped millions of women rise in their careers. She says that "care," the first four letters in the word "career," is her source of happiness.

3. **Time travel:** When you are on a mission, time is suspended. The clock ticks away, but what makes you tick knows no clock.

FROM POWERPOINT TO THE POINT OF POWER

I have been teaching business students for thirteen years how to move away from a PowerPoint to become the point of power. Slides are a distraction; the real attraction is *you*. Decks are not storytellers; you are.

Stories are food for our brains. Without them, we could not function. With them, we become part of a bigger story.

Acting is one of the best actions you can take at work. Act out a story to make a point. *New Yorker* cartoonist Roz Chast has developed an anatomy of a story in four parts: Once upon a time. Suddenly. Luckily. And happily ever after.

If you must use PowerPoint, try putting it in her appealing format. After a while, storytelling will come more naturally. And instead of your audience leaning back to check their phones, they will be leaning in to hear your every word.

ACTION IN LOVE

What would happen if you went to the soil and said, "Give me some fruit"?

The soil would respond, "Excuse me, but you're a little confused. You must be new. That's not how it works." The soil would explain that first you need to plant the seed and then you nurture—you water, fertilize, and protect it. And if you do these things well, you will be rewarded in due time with fruit. Otherwise, you could ask the soil forever, but it wouldn't change its way. You must keep giving and nurturing for the soil to bear fruit. Love grows the same way.

Love begins with loving yourself, with being good to your body, your mind, and your soul. Give yourself a hug right now. If that thought seems strange, that's all the more reason to do it. Most of us have been denied the person we need the most—ourselves. We desperately need to reestablish this relationship so we know how to have a positive relationship with someone else.

The typical childhood view of love is either nurturing or abusive, one we typically carry well into adulthood. My rule is whoever does not nurture you abuses you. Now, keep in mind that no one has had a perfect childhood unless their parents were dogs. That's as close to unconditional love as it gets. However, many people successfully resolve their past through self-exploration. Okay, you love yourself. Now you're going to share it with the luckiest person in the world: the person who loves you.

Based on the staggering divorce rate in this country, I think it's fair to say that most people *react* in their relationships rather than *act*. Here's a common scenario. "He" is taken aback by the horrible things "she" said. Instead of rubbing her back and helping her understand why she said it, he becomes angry and defensive. According to family therapist Esther Perel, the result is that people end up arguing with mistaken assumptions rather than allowing the other person to explain.

Most reactions are visitors from the past. Fears disguised as thoughts that make people say, "Well, that's just the way I am," or "You don't understand me." But most of the time you really don't understand you.

Action, on the other hand, means sharing your fears, dreams, and lives with one other. Action means sharing your soul. It also means having compassion and empathy for someone else. Being a friend of their excitement.

Love only works when we work on love. My twenty-four-year marriage is more than an act of love; it is taking actions 24/7 that grow that love. Psychologist and marriage counselor David Woodsfellow says that the number one predictor of a happy marriage is *the willingness to be influenced.* I asked him about the actions that supported this willingness. He offered four:

1. Listening

2. Understanding

3. Changing something

4. Knowing it's for the good of the relationship

Taken together, the first letters of each rule spell *luck.* It's a good way to remember how lucky we are to be in love and that the business of love never closes.

EMPATHY IS LOVE IN ACTION

Empathy is one of the keys to a great life. Empathy helps us stop judging and blaming others and understand them instead. Being empathetic to another person helps us see life through their lens, not just ours.

A friend told his fiancée that he wanted to share his life with her before they got married so he could see life through four eyes. Love is one of the ways to become more empathetic, which in turn nurtures love. This kind of love offers encouragement a heightened awareness and response to their needs. True love is when you truly see the other person. In this way, you both become a *we*, not two *I*'s.

SWINGING BACK INTO ACTION

Love isn't only about looking into one another's eyes; it's about looking in the same direction. My dear friend and psychologist Dr. Arthur Cohen and his wife Lois bought a swing for their backyard and for their relationship. For them, the swing represents peace at home. They are still swinging after fifty-five years of marriage.

Inspired, Cynthia and I also purchased a swing. We found that the Cohens were right. Rocking back and forth with the one you love creates a calming cadence. It will take you back to Troy in the fifth century B.C., where the swing was created as the symbol of play to be enjoyed after the conquest of war. It works. Some days feel like a battle. A simple swing can swing your side to victory. Cynthia and I now have two.

Actions talk. How many times have you been in a restaurant and watched two people share a table without sharing conversation? Could the food be so good? Or maybe their parents said, "No talking at the dinner table"? Here's a tip: If something is on your mind, spill the beans. Keeping it in or keeping your partner out will lead to heartburn and heartbreak. My mother used to say, "You are only as sick as your secrets." She was right. There are so many people who feel shame regarding a sickness, an addiction, or an abuse. Don't live with the injury. Share it with someone you trust.

WALK THE TALK

Talk about your life, your love, your children, your parents, your in-laws—just talk. Cynthia and I both have hectic schedules. Still, we meet at the same time and the same place every evening to share news about our jobs and to talk about how we're doing as a couple. Give yourself a checkup. Check on your lover. Check on your kids. Check on your parents. Check up. Check in, but don't check out.

Action in love also means demonstrating your love. Cynthia was a dedicated, determined, and dependable anchorwoman. She always got her story, and I knew she'd get this one.

In 1990, a report came over the wire about a pending drug bust in the penthouse of Atlanta's tallest building. Cynthia and her camera crew rushed to the scene of the crime. Surrounding the building were squads of police cars with lights flashing and a Red Dog SWAT team with machine guns loaded.

At first they wouldn't let Cynthia into the building, but like always, she persuaded them despite warnings that she was risking her life. Cynthia and a bulletproofed SWAT force took the elevator to the fiftieth floor, raced down the corridor, and broke through the door. But instead of finding a drug ring, she found me and an engagement ring.

She arrived thinking that she would get the "story of a lifetime." What she didn't know was that it would be her own.

HEALTH IN ACTION

Action leads to health. Inaction leads to hell. It's that simple. Moving is the first step to improving your health.

When you take action, you take destiny into your own hands. Still, many people have trouble marching forth when it comes to their health. Men, including me, are the worst. My wife and executive assistant had to coerce me into going for my annual checkup. The last one was five years ago.

Baby steps are the key to maintaining good health. Get the facts, get support. Get your buddy, your secretary, or your family to help you take positive action.

Pick a day. Your birthday. Your anniversary. How about March 4th?

Alcohol is making the world see double. If you think you drink too much, you probably do. If you don't have the courage to seek help, pick up a book on the "twelve steps." In fact, even if you've never had a drink, you ought to read about the twelve-step program anyway. I've been told that regardless of your addiction, the program will have you dancing back into life instead of falling into the substance.

Overweight people ought to throw out their diets. They're masochistic. Look at what the first three letters of *diet* spell: DIE. What heavy folks really need in their lives is more sugar—as in sweetness. The emptiness people feed with food can be fed with hobbies, movies, art classes, or yoga.

Most doctors agree that sugar is bad. So why not replace it with a different type of "sugar"? Hug yourself. Kiss the mirror. Tell yourself you're loved. You want to lose weight without losing your mind? Then stop thinking about losing and start thinking about gaining. New friends. New interests. A new goal. The stuff that will ultimately satisfy you can't be found in the fridge.

Exercise is action and it works. Moving at least three times a week allows you to enjoy three of life's luxuries: eating, drinking, and lovemaking. You don't have to bore yourself in the gym to burn. Dancing burns calories and puts you in the mood to take over the world. I try to dance at least once a day. Try it in your underwear at home with the music loud. And we're told that walking is one of the best things you can do for yourself. All good health is based on a state of well-being, so it's important to get motivated.

Now, get ready, because this might come as a shocker. Most people search all their lives for someone or something to get them motivated. A new hairdo. A new job. A new person. A new passion. A new way to live life. The irony is that you will never be motivated unless you take action first. <u>Underline</u> this: First you take action, then you get motivated. Not the other way around.

GOD IN ACTION

Perhaps the greatest action we can take is to move toward faith. It doesn't matter what religion you are. It doesn't even matter if you have a religion. What matters is believing. Faith is the only thing in the world that never changes.

When my hand was paralyzed after the car accident, the priest who came into my hospital room was surely heaven sent. Though I am Jewish, he prayed sincerely for me. I will never forget the feeling of faith I had as I fell asleep that night. Nor will I forget the feeling I had in my fingers the next morning. Though full recovery was more than a year away, I had experienced a miracle—faith. It is greater than any religion our world has to offer, because it is not of this world.

An interesting sidebar to this story is that I met a Jewish boy from Virginia in that Italian hospital who had suffered a ruptured appendix. While I was fortunate to have my mother by my side, his parents were not there. This sixteen-year-old was scared, so my mother and I took care of him. We gave him much-needed faith. When he was ready to leave, not knowing that I, too, was Jewish, he told me, "I never knew Christians were so loving."

I said, "Thank you."

When you give someone a hand, you are as close to being godlike as you can be in this lifetime, because your good deed is really God's action. The more you give to others, the more divine you become. Marlo Thomas has spent a lifetime raising money and hope for the kids at St. Jude Children's Research Hospital. Her father, the legendary Danny Thomas, believed that there are two kinds of people in this world, the takers and the givers. He said, "The takers may eat a little better, but the givers sleep a little better." Whether you use your hand to create a little garden, write a check to your favorite charity, or wipe away someone's tears, no action is bigger or more sacred. It's the little things we do that mean so much.

Action is the journey from *know thyself* to *go thyself*. For when a human being becomes a human doing, she or he can feel the real rapture of life. The beauty is that the doing need not be big. In fact, as the next chapter will show, a little goes a long way.

FINGER TIPS

- The plural of U is Us.

- When you're in love, the whole world is spiritual.

- The best handheld is a hand held.

- Rather than using PowerPoint, be the point of power.

- March forth on your dream.

- The word "career" starts with the word "care."

- Being perfect is an imperfect goal.

- Better to make it count than to count what you made.

- Baseball is our national pastime because the game is about getting home and being safe.

- Your presence is the best of all presents.

CHAPTER 5

LITTLE IS
THE NEW BIG

Little things take so little energy for
all the good they produce. Only when
we recognize the little things can we
understand the bigger picture, and only
when we do little things for others can
we appreciate how truly big we are.

Ending on the littlest finger is no accident. My pinky delivered the biggest lesson—that every journey is made up of little steps. For me, the return of sensation to my pinky was the biggest Thumbs Up of all. It meant my hand was whole. The doctors concurred. With lots of physical therapy, I would achieve 100 percent use of my right hand and arm. Little was the new big.

Little is how we all begin. As children we make pinky swears—do-or-die promises between friends. As an adult, my pinky now serves as a promise to myself to cherish those little things and moments that add up to a rich life.

Little actions enlarge and enrich our lives. A word of encouragement, a wistful wink, a soft touch, a forgiving thought, a kind gesture, a little prayer are messengers of hope.

Little things don't cost much but they are invaluable. A handwritten thank you at the bottom of your rent check. A note tucked into your spouse's briefcase or lunch bag. A text to your favorite teacher after a great class. A sunset with someone you love. Paying the toll for the driver behind you. Forgiving someone you said you would never forgive.

Little things amaze. Requiring minimal energy, they deliver maximum impact. In recognizing the small wonders, we begin to grasp the world at large. Small acts for others demonstrate how truly big we can be. Even praying a little helps us feel the hand of God.

Ironically, we are taught to accomplish big things, but it's the little ones that count. Moments along the way create momentum in our lives, which in turn can create a life that is momentous.

LITTLE GROWS BIG

Ralph Waldo Emerson wrote, "The creation of a thousand forests is in one acorn," which reminds me of *A Sound of Thunder* by Ray Bradbury, a story about a time traveler, Eckels, who lives in the year 2055. One day he traveled back millions of years to get a glimpse of the dinosaurs. Time travel rules stated that he could not step off the designated path. He saw plenty of prehistoric life, though in his excitement he stepped off the path and squashed a butterfly.

When Eckels returned to the year 2055, he realized the death of the butterfly, which had seemed small, caused a series of events changing his environment and the future in a big way—even altering the outcome of an election, 65 million years later.

Life works the same way as "the butterfly effect." Little things beget big things. A meeting, a memo, even a small memento can change your destiny.

LITTLE THINGS CAN HAVE BIG MEANING

In 1941 the German Jewish psychiatrist Viktor Frankl had to make a big decision: Should he stay in Vienna to take care of his aging parents or flee to the United States to escape the Nazis?

Looking for a hint from heaven, he was rewarded. Upon visiting his family's home, Frankl found a memento from a synagogue that had been leveled by the Nazis. It was a piece of rubble—a fragment from a copy of the Ten Commandments. It said, *Honor thy mother and father*. With that sign, he stayed and served his parents.

Unfortunately, Frankl was sent to a concentration camp. As prisoner #119104, Frankl helped his fellow inmates face the horrors of the Holocaust. In doing so, he discovered that having a purpose determined whether you would survive or perish.

My favorite book, *Man's Search For Meaning,* was Frankl's testament to the power of this greater meaning in our lives. By encouraging us to search for meaning over money, he touched millions of lives, including mine.

Some time ago, a big company wanted to buy out my agency. It would have made me a very wealthy man, but there was a catch. I would have to give up the name BrightHouse and my company's purpose— to brighten the world of business. I did lots of soul searching.

Staring out at the clouds while on a flight to New York to meet my suitor, I, too, asked for a sign from heaven. Reaching into the seat pocket in front of me for a magazine, I found instead a book that someone had left behind. It was *Man's Search For Meaning,* and it ended my search for an answer.

THE LITTLEST DIAMOND SHINES THE BRIGHTEST

My maternal grandmother, Mae, lived 103 years, but at age fifty, she thought her life was over. It was the 1950s and she was getting a divorce. At the time the "D" word was a stigma that said you had failed. She felt shame, hurt, and anger, and she was practically broke. My mother encouraged her to take a trip and leave her worries behind. So she did.

On her fateful train ride to St. Louis, a man named Harry asked if he could join her for lunch. She agreed and a delicious conversation ensued. By the time they reached St. Louis, they had agreed to have dinner there. That meal led to more meals and another city, New York, where Harry took Mae dancing.

Whoops—Mae broke her heel while dancing. Harry told her not to worry, that he could get another pair of shoes around the corner. "But it's nearly midnight," she said.

Harry and Mae arrived at a swanky shoe store called Chandlers on Fifth Avenue. He took a key from his pocket and opened the store's Lalique doors. My grandmother was stunned. "Can you get in trouble for this?" she asked.

He answered, "No worries, Mazie," as he had started to call her. "Pick out any pair. I work here and I get a special discount. I will let the store manager know tomorrow." She chose a pair and she and Harry returned to the dance floor.

A three-month courtship followed. One evening after dining at a New York City coffee shop, Harry proposed, offering Mae a tiny sliver of a diamond. When Mae gave him a big yes, Harry pulled out a Tiffany box and bedazzled his intended with a spectacular five-carat diamond in a platinum setting.

Turns out Harry was Harry Edison of Edison Brothers of St. Louis, the largest shoe business in the world at the time. The company owned many shoe chains, including Chandlers. This piece of family history reminds me that little happenstances like breaking a heel can lead to life's most priceless gems.

THE LITTLEST BIG SPEECH

Being optimistic is an attitude. Reaching altitude takes pointing to your purpose and having the courage to take action. Your deed need not be big. One small gesture can have a large and lasting impact.

I was to give a speech in Atlanta during a rainstorm of biblical proportion. Instead of the 200 people we expected, one woman sat alone in the audience. I told my publicist and then-agent, Robyn Spizman, who had accompanied me to the talk, that I would apologize to the lady and call off the speech. No way was I going to stand up and give an hour talk to one person.

Robyn saw things differently. "You are booked. You have an audience and that woman is going to hear the greatest speech of her life," she told me.

Unnerved, I walked out on stage and did my best to deliver to her heart what I had in mine.

At the end of the talk, I heard the sound of two hands clapping. They belonged to Robyn. The woman in the audience had left without a word.

On the way home I lamented to Robyn how tough it was to give a talk to someone who was busy writing in her notebook the whole time and how disappointing it was that she left silently. Six months later, however, I received a letter from that very same woman recounting that evening and the months that followed. She wanted me to know that the speech about *the hand* had changed her life. The woman had written down as much as she could, confident that the words were meant just for her. The next day she started to make positive changes in her life. She told me, "Due to loving, not just living, my life, my cancer has gone into remission."

I will forever remember the littlest speech I ever gave as my biggest.

A LITTLE T.L.C.

There is nothing more powerful than the combination of tenderness, love, and care. To be tender is to protect as a tender mother, to express gentle emotion with a tender glance, and to be soft with a tender heart. Tender also means fragile, which we all are at one time or another.

Remember the common shipping instruction: *Fragile. Handle with care.* Showing love is how we share our tenderness. Not keeping how you feel to yourself but being affectionate. Caring is using your deep knowledge of another to help them grow. When it comes to kindness and a little T.L.C., always default to yes.

A LITTLE PRESENCE

Much has been written about the rewards of living in the moment. But being present by yourself is not nearly as cool as being fully present for someone you love. This is hard to do while tethered to technology, as so many of us are.

In 2013 I wrote a fun article for LittlePinkBook.com titled "10 BlackBerry Commandments." These rules for connection apply equally to all mobile devices. The commandments ranged from "Thou shall not take the BlackBerry to any table with food or family since a BlackBerry is not a fruit, nor does it come from a tree" to "Thou shall not BlackBerry in lieu of responding to a child's request (e.g., 'Wait a second, I'm reading something.')."

Never let tech take the place of touch. Presence is all about staying in touch, being in touch, and creating touching moments or peak moments, as I like to call them. Peak moments are magical little snippets of time that come about when you and others are so present, so in touch, so in sync, so on the same page, and so full of joy that you feel perfect harmony.

Relationships are like pianos. They need to be tuned every day. Do this and your relationship will sing. How do you do this? Stay tuned in to your partner's thoughts, desires, and frustrations. Most important, be a friend of his or her excitement.

Today can only be joyful if we are joy-filled. And the only way to be filled with joy is to fill another with joy. Who will you fill with joy today?

A LITTLE WORD OF ENCOURAGEMENT

Grandma Mae became a rich woman in many ways when she met Harry. She was able to pay for my college education, something my parents could not do. I attended Brandeis University, where I majored in

American Studies. It was a default major for someone like myself who had no compelling interests. That was the case until I wrote a paper for one of my courses, Class Struggle in America. Unlike my peers, who wrote well-researched papers on the subject, I had a different idea.

My thesis statement was, "If you're wealthy and born Christian, you aspire to become Jewish. If you're wealthy and born Jewish, you aspire to become Christian." I received a B+ with the following note from the professor: "Joey, your quantitative data leaves me with big questions and your conclusion is far-fetched, if not preposterous. But boy, can you write!"

Those last five words changed my life. I had been given a thumbs up. With the stroke of another's pen, I had become a writer.

What words of encouragement are you giving to those who need it most?

The word "encouragement" has the same root as the word "courage." It is from the Old French word *courage,* which means heart. So when we give encouragement, we are giving heart to another person.

A LITTLE WORD OF CAUTION

The word "character" comes from the Greek word *karakter*, which means an engraved mark or imprint on the soul. When someone speaks ill of another, they leave a mark on that person's reputation. One little word that wrongs another can strike as hard as a fist.

There is a story about a New York City man who gossiped wrongly about his neighbor. Unfortunately, he did not do his research. The man he maligned was a *mensch*, which is the Yiddish word for a person with a strong moral and ethical sense.

Feeling guilty, the man called to apologize for the inaccurate communication. "Meet me atop the Empire State Building," the gentleman said, "and we will talk about it."

The two men met. The neighbor came with a down pillow. He said, "My friend, a man's reputation is like a feathered pillow. When you cut him, you cut the pillow." At that moment, he tore open the pillow and thousands of feathers flew across Manhattan. "To put that reputation back together," he said, "is no less difficult than to get all those feathers back in the pillow."

I believe that most people don't do wrong but are wronged. Remember the golden rule: *Do unto others as you would have them do unto you*. Better yet, do unto others as *they* would have you do unto *them*. That is real empathy. It's easy to criticize others. What takes real talent is lifting others up.

A LITTLE UNDERSTANDING

One of the most valuable gems I have acquired along my life journey is the knowledge that I cannot change people—I can only try to understand them better. Through the lens of understanding we see people more clearly and dearly. What's more, they see us as friends who want to understand them rather than judge them.

Try it. Think about someone in your life—it might even be you—whom you have judged. Now put on your understanding hat and feel what happens. When you know people, you grow people.

Imagine if warring countries practiced understanding one another rather than judging each other. The promise of peace would be closer at hand, just as it is with people we try to understand.

A LITTLE NOTE ABOUT HOW I MET YOUR MOTHER

The body's tiniest response can have huge consequences. Take blinking. Your eyes blink 60,000 times a day without a thought, protecting the eyes and keeping them moist. But what happens when you want to send a message to someone with a wink?

You put purpose into a blink and the blink becomes a wink!

My first date with Cynthia was actually a blind date. We ate breakfast together at the Ritz-Carlton in October 1989. We both ordered eggs and stared into each other's eyes. Then I winked and Cynthia winked back. Those two little winks led to romance, marriage, two amazing children, two horses, three chickens, two parakeets, and Lucy the cat.

A LITTLE THING THAT LED US HOME

When my wife and I began searching for a house, we were shown a grand Tudor full of intricate detail and hand-carved moldings. The agent almost had us sold, but we couldn't get past the fact that this Hogwarts-like house sat on a lot of less than a quarter acre. In a last-ditch effort to sell us, the agent said, "You and Cynthia are a prince and a princess; you need a castle. Not some little cottage like the one down the block."

That little comment led to us buy that "little cottage," which sits on two beautiful acres, that we still live in twenty-four years later.

A LITTLE FASHION ADVICE

Nurses' outfits say healing. Firemen's outfits say protecting. Your outfits say, "This is me." So if you want to be the best you, take a trip to your closet.

Pick out your favorite outfits and wear only those. Our favorite outfits make us feel and become more confident.

A LITTLE MEASURE OF WONDER

We grow the way we are measured. How are you measured? If it's by your net worth, your self-worth will suffer. If you're measured by how you look, you may be admired today but will lose face tomorrow. If it is by your power, that, too, will pass.

Here's my rule of thumb: By age sixty-five you will have had the potential to witness more than 200,000 sunsets. My wife and I keep track of how many sunsets we have seen. At the writing of this book, we have seen 525 full sunsets, and nine of them presented us with the green flash. When conditions are just right, a green ray of sunshine is visible above the upper rim of the disk of the sun for a second or two. But for us, it lasts longer because that green light is a GO sign. It says go on, go for it, go for broke, and go for the gold. It says raise your thumb in praise of this daily miracle.

Find your sunset tonight. As the sun bows to earth, know this: Behind our torment is beauty, ready and waiting to make its debut.

My idea of people who measure up has changed, too. When I was younger I admired clever people. Now in my sixties, I look up to kind people. Kindness is everything. It has more value than any material gift, because it cannot be bought.

Sure, it's nice to be important. But it's more important to be nice.

A LITTLE PRICELESS

How much do you think the following things would cost if you had to buy them? What would you pay to see a flower bloom, to skip a rock across a lake, or to sit under the stars? I remember on one of our first dates my wife took me to Mulholland Drive in Los Angeles, near where she grew up. We were sitting in her convertible and she told me to close my eyes, stand up, and put my hand out. She moved it up ever so slightly.

"Open your eyes," she commanded. There sitting atop my outstretched hand was the fullest moon I had ever seen.

"I give you this moon, Joey," she memorably said.

A LITTLE GESTURE

Sometimes one gesture can kick-start a life. I remember trying out for the swim team in junior high school. I was not an especially good student, so I thought sports might be my thing. Turns out I was not an especially good swimmer, either.

I had a crush on a girl who would come to my swim trials. Just before my qualifying meet, I saw her in the stands. A second before the starting pistol went off, she gave me a thumbs up. Bang. I set a school record that day. More important, I set a course for myself and learned that a little gesture can lead to a big life.

A LITTLE GIFT

Here is a gift. It might seem a little weird, but I promise it works. The next time you buy something for yourself, have it gift-wrapped. When you get home, leave your present on the dining room table. Then go out. When you come back home and open the door, I guarantee that you will smile. Look, there's a present and it's just for you!

A LITTLE MORNING RITUAL

We all know what happens when we wake up on the wrong side of the bed. Let me share a trick I use to get going in the right direction. Go to the carpet store and buy a small remnant of red carpet. Before going to sleep at night, place the carpet near your bed so you step on it first thing in the morning. It might not feel like sashaying down the red carpet in Hollywood, but it will send a message to your brain that today, and every day, you deserve red carpet treatment.

A LITTLE LIKE IS CONTAGIOUS

When we sign up for Facebook, we agree to let them use our data to improve their service. Back in 2012, Facebook conducted an experiment. They sent 600,000 users a news report that was not true but was of a positive nature. Then they transmitted a negative one. Facebook assessed the posts that followed. Guess what? Those who received positive news sent positive news to their friends, while those who got negative reports conveyed thumbs-down messages to their contacts.

Good is viral. Take the phenomenon of the ALS Ice Bucket Challenge. Amyotrophic lateral sclerosis is a devastating neurodegenerative disease that often leaves its victims totally paralyzed.

In 2014, the ALS Association created the ALS Ice Bucket Challenge. People all over the world, including Oprah and dozens of other celebrities, poured a bucket of ice water over their heads and challenged others to do the same or make a donation to fight ALS. Many people did both. The ALS Association soaked up nearly $100 million in donations and close to 2.5 million videos were splashed over the internet.

The challenge worked because liking is contagious, especially so when it's about a positive cause. One thing you can be positive about is that every plus multiplies.

Think of the mint on the pillow. When hotels place a morsel of chocolate on the bed, it creates a like. Enough likes turn into love. Try a like today. Place a Hershey's Kiss on your partner's keyboard, a sweet note on the steering wheel, or a flower on the pillow.

A LITTLE WORD MAKES A BIG DIFFERENCE

"And" kicks "but." That's because "and" builds and "but" is an obstacle. "And" is a go; "but" is a stop. Next time you are talking, try replacing "but" with "and"— see what happens. Remember, it's not what you say, it's what people hear.

Another power-packed word is "great." Tell someone they are great and you can turn their world right-side up. Try:

"Great job!"

"You are a great communicator!"

"That project turned out great."

And how about the butt-kicking word, "imagine"?! Especially when used at the beginning of a sentence, "imagine" is the key that unlocks your imagination, an open invitation to think as big as you wish. Listen to John Lennon sing "Imagine." Then imagine the world for yourself.

A LITTLE SOMETHING TO SLEEP ON

Turns out that a little snooze is a big deal. We are built to have two rest cycles. Those circadian rhythms peak twice every twenty-four hours, so the second cycle lands in the middle of the afternoon. A siesta after lunch improves alertness, memory, creativity, and even your sex life, while reducing the chance of burnout and heart attack.

Painter Salvador Dalí would hold a spoon in his hand as he dozed. When the spoon dropped from his hand to the floor he was done. Just fifteen minutes in dreamland can replace that energy drink and refresh your body, mind, and spirit. I know it's hard to grab some shuteye in a world that won't shut down, but finding a little time and a little place in your office to rest your head will keep you ahead of the rest.

A LITTLE MOVEMENT

I'm a Baby Boomer, part of the post–World War II baby boom born between 1946 and 1964. My generation is often characterized by our stuff, the things we've accumulated over the years. The trouble for many is that you can't get enough of what you don't need. I have yet to see a U-Haul behind a hearse.

I often think of my generation not as Boomers but *Kaboomers*—people whose lives went kaboom when they finally realized that things don't bring happiness, people do.

In retrospect, it was the little things that made the biggest impact on my life. The first Father's Day card from my son, the first Father's Day card from both of my sons, love letters from my wife, and emails from my students telling me that the class I teach at Emory University has changed their lives.

So there is hope for Boomers who became Kaboomers. We can start loving people and using things instead of using people. Then, the original flower children can call themselves *Bloomers*.

A LITTLE AD-VICE

Ads can be a vice. I spent twenty years in advertising selling people optical illusions. More than $500 billion is spent every year by advertisers trying to convince people to spend money they don't have on things they don't need to impress people they don't know.

Ads don't add up. That's why I left my *Mad Men* world to pursue a career in creating *glad* men and women in the business world, working for executives who believe that good and service trump goods and services.

Imagine your life untainted by the 10,000 media messages you are bombarded with every day. Here is how you do it: Subtract the ad. If you still like the product or service, buy it. I bet if you do, it will be the result of little positive actions that companies are taking to make your world a little better. Little acts of kindness, such as sponsoring a charity walk or supplying free products to those in need, are the ads of the future.

A LITTLE WALK CAN GO A LONG WAY

The poet Wallace Stevens wrote, "Perhaps the truth depends on a walk around the lake." Interestingly, Steve Jobs held walking meetings. He believed that walking was as important as talking, and when you put them together, you produce better solutions.

At BrightHouse, we have an expression inspired by the inventor and polymath Leonardo da Vinci: *Learn your craft and walk away.* So during creative working sessions, we don't take breaks, we take *walk-aways.* Putting distance between what you did and what can be done brings new ideas closer. You will find that walking away even for a moment can lead to discovery. A stroll gets you on a roll. And if you want to feel six feet higher than you do right now, take a walk through the nearest cemetery.

A LITTLE BREATH OF FRESH AIR

"Yoga" means union. And that is what happens on the mat. When you do yoga, your body, mind, and spirit unionize. Do it enough and that feeling of union becomes part of your life. When union becomes part of your every day, the biggest lie in life is revealed: that we are separate from one another. Separateness takes us apart. Yoga puts us back together.

At the center of yoga practice is the breathing that centers us. This breathing gives us a glimpse into the powerful union of a clear mind, a stretched body, and a strong spirit—the most important "muscle" in the human body.

The poses are challenging, but I have found that breathing through them creates calm and cuts through anxiety. Remember, the word "inspire" is from the Latin *inspirare*, which means to breathe. Throughout the day, I will take a deep breath and hold it for a count of three. Exhale at the count of eight. Do it again and again. Remind yourself that three-eight rhymes with create.

Invest in a yoga class and learn how to breathe. Until I did, breathing was something that I took for granted. Now it grants me a little peace and harmony.

A LITTLE HOMEWORK

Go to the place where you feel most comfortable. It might be a dance studio, an orchard, a park, the lake, the ocean, your school, or your home.

This place of comfort is where your light lives. It's the joy in your heart. Your job from this day forward is to take that light to all the places in your life. When you bring home to work, you will have completed your *homework*.

A LITTLE WISDOM

The wisest people on earth are often those who have been here the longest—our elders. After age forty we lose about a half inch of height every decade. So ironically, as time goes by, people get little. But our oldest have the tallest order: to pass down what keeps us up. How do they do it? The clock has not always given them a kind hand.

While writing this book, I visited a nursing home in Atlanta. The third floor is the Alzheimer's unit. They keep the doors secure so patients don't wander off. What happens instead is that these people wander off in their minds as they sit, often in wheelchairs.

I pulled up a chair to chat with a former Navy airship pilot, ninety-three-year-old Jack, or Honey as he is called by those who adore him, which is everyone. His wife of sixty-seven years, Phyllis, holds his hand in hers. Alzheimer's is like a mental lost and found. You lose your memory, which is everything, and then you find it for a moment.

I am lucky enough to have witnessed one of those moments. Phyllis asked, "Do you love me?" Honey smiled at his bride and sang, "More than a bushel and a peck and a hug around the neck." Then Honey gave me a thumbs up, a gesture firmly embedded in his mind. That is the secret of life from a man whose mind wanders but whose heart and positive outlook are firmly grounded.

And here is proof that wisdom comes with age. When I was twenty-one my eighty-year-old grandfather, Opa, told me, "There's nothing in life like a good scare." He was talking about that feeling you get when you think you are sick and anticipate the worst. Then you find out you are okay and you vow a new lease on life.

"Suddenly, the world looks so fresh and you count your blessings. Why must we scare ourselves into being happy and thankful?" Opa asked. "Instead, what if we lived as if we are going to die? Which we will. So how about treasuring every day as if it were our last?" They were not his last words, but they certainly lasted with me.

A LITTLE STORY ABOUT THIS STORY

Let me share a story about how this book came about. It was 1986. I had ordered new checks from my bank, but they never arrived. They were delivered instead to well-known Atlanta author, book promoter, and daughter of Honey, Robyn Spizman. When she saw my name on the checks, she remembered a speech that I had given.

Robyn came to my office with my checks and a plan to turn my talk about being Thumbs Up into a book. Almost three decades later, I still keep one of those checks framed to remind me that we write our own check for the amount of good fortune we want in our lives.

Looking back, I know it was not a postal mix-up. It was a special delivery. As the Italian poet Dante put it, "From a little spark bursts a mighty flame."

A LITTLE PEACE OF BUSINESS

Business is now part of every human endeavor, so how should commerce redefine its new and important role in the world? Perhaps the answer is in the root of the word "competition," from the Latin *competere,* which means to thrive together.

"Purpose" is the mantra of my global consultancy, BrightHouse, which has built a reputation on the powerful notion that greater purpose in business can make the world a brighter place. If it takes a village to raise a child, it takes many capable leaders to elevate a company. People who have each other's backs are always in front of their competitors. Everyone needs support to step out into a complex and an often unforgiving world. Knowing they are part of a band of brothers and sisters is gratifying and exciting.

Having all we need paves the way for giving others what they need. This takes business from a myopic focus on the bottom line to the front lines of the world where the terrors of inhumanity and inequality play out. The question becomes, "Now that the world is burning, what must business do?"

The answer is the shift from sustaining the life of business to inspiring the business of life. Then, commerce will dedicate itself to the highest levels of humanity—to do no harm, to stand in harm's way, and to make way for an era of caring, compassionate, peace-filled commerce.

When big business is the goal, bigness is the result. What if the dream of business were instead more peace in the world? I am not suggesting that your P&L should stand for "Peace & Love," but we grow the way we are measured. If business's yardstick were how happy it could make the world, we would have new economic indicators. Take a look at the country of Bhutan, which has moved from measuring GDP (Gross Domestic Product) to measuring GNH (Gross National Happiness). It takes into account psychological well-being, health, education, time use, cultural diversity, resilience, good governance, community vitality, ecological diversity, and living standards.

When we learn that peace in business is more valuable than winning your next piece of business, the world of business will have truly won.

A LITTLE EMPATHY

Empathy is to be one with another's feelings. McGill University empathy expert Anita Nowak asked me to imagine that I'm passing by a person who is in a hole and trying to get out. If I pass by the hole to look down at the person, Nowak told me, that is pity. If I feel badly for him, that is sympathy. If I give him a sandwich because I think he might be hungry down in that hole, that is compassion.

But if I get down in the hole and help the person climb out, we are talking empathy. I experienced this firsthand as the person in the hole when I fell into depression. My wife Cynthia crawled down into my pit with no pity. And she took what Nowak calls *empathic action*. Her deep listening, constancy of love, and devotion to being present for me were the rungs on my ladder out of that hole.

Feeling pity is like stepping on people. Feeling empathy is living in their shoes. The path to empathy is not to think of others as others. Othering destroys empathy. The only way to empathy is feeling another's feelings as our own, as if we were saving ourselves.

Empathy is the glue of great relationships. It creates a bond of trust where each person feels the other has his or her back. Each supports the other's dreams. And each knows they are safe and secure. Each becomes number two to the other. The result is that the relationship becomes number one.

A LITTLE PRESENT ON YOUR BIRTHDAY

My grandfather Opa lived until he was eighty-eight years old. I will never forget his birthday parties, because no one was allowed to bring presents. He used to say that birthdays were not for presents but for celebrating being loved and being present. So, instead of collecting gifts, he would give each of us a present in gratitude for being a part of his life.

A LITTLE ATTENTION BEATS A TON OF INTENTION

Relationships thrive when we are attentive to each other. As I learned over the last twenty-four years of my marriage, our good intentions never worked as well as fulfilling each other's little requests.

These little requests, like getting your partner a cup of coffee or turning off the light, are about going that extra mile or, in most cases, just an extra inch. These little things are bids for attention. Be sure to turn toward each other when they are made, and chances are you'll have it made.

A LITTLE PEBBLE GOES A LONG WAY

Building the life you have always dreamed about can be daunting. My mother had a way of looking at big things that took the hugeness out of them. She said, "There are no rocks, just little pebbles."

By looking at the biggest problems in our lives as lots of little ones, we can imagine checking them off our list rather than feeling overwhelmed. The next time a boulder is headed at you, be bolder by knowing it's just an optical illusion. That's not a big rock ahead of you—just lots of little pebbles.

A LITTLE COOKING
LESSON FROM SICILY

While on a family vacation in Sicily, we had the honor of taking a cooking lesson from a well-known local chef. What we learned was not only how to make cavatelli and Sicilian meatballs, but the recipe for a delicious life.

Our chef sees Sicily as "a salad of people" from many parts of the world. Though she admonishes those past cultures that took from Sicily, she is also grateful for the contributions, most importantly the cuisine, that they left behind.

First there were the Greeks and Romans, who loved a banquet, the precursor to the family-style table. They also cherished salt so much they paid their soldiers with it, hence the word "salary" from the Latin *salarium*.

Then came the Arabs, who brought rice, sugar, and seasonings to Sicilian dining, making garlic famous. Following were the Spanish, including many monks and nuns who spent their days praying and cooking, both godsends to Sicilians.

Enter the French, who offered up pastries that would inspire the likes of the cannoli and tiramisu. Last, the New World travelers from America garnished Sicilian dishes with tomatoes and potatoes.

By the end of our lesson we had learned one thing: Against common wisdom, there can never be too many cooks in the kitchen. There are no lone creators. Only legions of people create legends.

Michelangelo had more than twenty artisans paint the Sistine Chapel. Walt Disney had more than 700 animators work on each of his films. Sicily is famous for its food because of what diverse people and cultures brought to the table.

Each of us doing our little part makes for the feast of life.

A LITTLE WORD

I offer a cure for the cold. One word, my favorite word, is a word that, though virtually obsolete, will help us come in from the cold. That word is "apricity."

Apricity is the warmth of the sun breaking through in winter. Coming from the Latin word *apricus* meaning "to be warmed by the sun," apricity is what I suggest we practice with each other and ourselves.

Warmth is affection, a gentle feeling of fondness. When we are kind and tender to others, that warmth breaks through and heals their cold. We connect. When we care for ourselves, our hearts are warmed.

Imagine a world of apricity—a place where the warmth of the sun on our skin inspires us to feel more alive, enthusiastic, kind, and connected.

THINK PINKY

Have you ever had your day turn around because of one kind word or gesture? Here are ten little things that can change the direction of your day and, who knows, maybe your destiny!

1. **SMILE:** Walk out the door smiling. A smile is the most powerful tool in building goodwill, good times, good memories, and good in the world. If you are lucky you will get a smile back. It takes one more muscle to smile than to frown. But that one muscle can rock someone's world.

2. **CALL:** Many years ago I created *the forgiving phone* for a famous spa. The phone sat on a pedestal at the top of a mountain, and callers could call anywhere in the world as long as the call was to forgive someone. Call someone today and forgive. Forgiving is for giving. And there's another benefit: That person is no longer living rent free in your head!

3. **WRITE:** Five thousand years ago, a person writing a thank-you letter had to find some clay, then chisel words onto the wet clay, bake it in the sun, and send a messenger to ride a day or two to deliver it. Today, in the age of easy emails and text

messages, a handwritten note means just as much. In fact, the effort you put in is as important as the content you put out.

4. **HUG:** I learned in Mexico that you must always hug someone to the right so your heart touches the heart of the other person. I learned from my mother that you should always be the last one to let go. And I learned from my wife that cuddling makes a little hug huge.

5. **GARDEN:** It's called a flowerbed because this is where beauty sleeps. To awaken it, just pick a flower. Picked flowers pick people up. Send eleven flowers to someone you love with this message: *You are number twelve.*

6. **BAKE:** Something made by hand is worth more than a handful of money. My grandmother Oma, who was married to Opa, made cakes and cookies for those she loved. Every time I walked into her kitchen, I felt loved.

   This is Oma's special Vanilla Almond Crescent recipe from Vienna, Austria:

   1¼ cups flour

   ¾ cup butter

   ½ cup blanched and grated almonds

2 egg yolks

⅓ cup sugar

¼ cup vanilla sugar

Work flour, butter, almonds, egg yolks, and sugar into a dough. Form small crescents and bake at 300° F for fifteen to twenty minutes. While cookies are still hot, dip them into vanilla sugar to coat.

Made (vs. paid) is the secret ingredient.

7. **VOLUNTEER:** The opposite of good is not evil, it is indifference. There is more to life than having it all. It's called giving your all. When we give of ourselves, a life with cause is life with effect.

8. **CHANGE:** If you want to change the world, change your daily routine. Routines turn into ruts and eventually graves. So change the way you go to work today. Change the way you come home. Change the way you say hello to your spouse or partner. Announce that the luckiest person in the world is home. Change things up and in no time things will look up.

9. **TRUST:** Every successful relationship is based on trust. The fastest way to find out if you can trust people is to give them

your trust. Find a person today and put your trust in him or her. That break could lead to a breakthrough relationship.

10. **PRAY:** I talk to God at least once a day. But I listen to God more than a dozen times throughout the day. All you have to do is be silent.

GIVE YOUR HEART AND MIND A LITTLE HAND

We have taken an amazing journey together. One that started with a simple idea—that being Thumbs Up is at the heart of everything. From there we learned how to fill our minds with purpose, empty our fears, take action on our good thoughts, and that a little can help you make it big.

Now it's time to take what was born in your heart and grew up in your mind and put it to work with your hands. This was Gandhi's wish for humankind: *to build a better self so you could build a better world.*

We feed our bodies food and our minds knowledge, but our spirits are often starving. The name Gandhi means "grocer." Our spirits hunger for something greater and that something is kindness. For humankind to prosper we need kind humans.

Just like 60 million years ago, it all starts with one little gesture. Thumb meets finger and the rest, as they say, is history.

FINGER TIPS

When we are without everything, we are everything.

The word "ill" begins with "I." The word "well" begins with "we."

People without patience become patients.

Humankind will survive because of kind humans.

Love the world as yourself and you will embrace everyone.

LOVE. Everything else is a consolation prize.

EPILOGUE

JOINING HANDS CREATES COMMUNITY

As you turn these final pages, I offer one final thought. I wrote this book not just to hand down my wisdom but to tell you that you already have in hand what you need to be happy. Like our hands and fingers, we are emotionally wired to connect. We are born to hold onto and reach out to those around us.

But before we can connect with others, we must connect with ourselves. We have to give *ourselves* the thumbs up.

A thumb was in the air during so many great moments in history. Whether it was the Beatles arriving in our country or Franklin Roosevelt saving it, an astronaut leaving earth, or a soldier returning from battle, a raised thumb raised spirits and elevated hopes.

The word "existence" comes from the Latin word *existere*, meaning to emerge. That is the work of purpose. As you find yours, a new life will emerge. It is a journey and will take time, but it begins with a feather of hope, even a thought.

Life works when you find your life's work—the thing that makes you tick. The philosopher Friederich Nietzsche wrote, "He who has a *why* to live for can deal with almost any *how*." I would add that when you have a *why*, you have a reason for *being*, and *doing* will become a pleasure.

No one said life was easy. Fear and uncertainty stand in our way. But when we realize that fear is not real, it's easier to deal with the setbacks when they come. Rose Kennedy, who suffered great personal loss during her lifetime, reminded us, "Birds sing after a storm; why shouldn't people feel as free to delight in whatever remains to them?"

She kept marching forth. And that is our choice and privilege as human beings, not in the pursuit of perfection but in the name of progress. We are all works in progress. Our job is to create ourselves so we can create a kinder, more loving world.

Ours is the little planet where big things happen, like standing shoulder to shoulder, recognizing that everyone who has ever lived is connected by the need to love and be loved.

After the Nobel Prize–winning biologist George Wald received his award, he said, "What one really needs is not Nobel laureates but love. How do you think one gets to be a Nobel laureate? Wanting love, that's how. Wanting it so bad one works all the time and ends up a Nobel laureate. It's a consolation prize. What matters is love."

In my son Julien's high school thesis, he wrote, "Even in war, soldiers fall to the ground and hug the earth, only to be connected one last time."

Connect to those you love. Reach out to those in pain who need help and healing. Hold onto the reins of life, as the ride can be bumpy and filled with challenges. You are the solution architect of your life. Hold tightly and don't let go.

Thank you for taking my hand. Now, take yours and create the life you have always dreamed about. I hope this handbook will help you hold on to your dreams by living them, pointing you in the right direction by keeping your heart and mind focused, helping you overcome your fears by grasping faith, and encouraging you to think bigger by recognizing life's most precious little things, including each other. Most important, I hope it shows you that if you follow this blueprint, life really works.

Everyone is looking for answers out there. You hold them all in your hand. So let your hand be a constant reminder from this day forth that if you want something, anything, all you have to do is pick it up. But begin by picking yourself up first.

Now, give yourself a big hand!

RESOURCES

If you have enjoyed *Thumbs Up*, please contact me:
jreiman@thinkbrighthouse.com

BrightHouse US Website:
www.thinkbrighthouse.com

BrightHouse Brasil Website:
www.brighthousebrasil.com.br

Join our purpose-powered community:
www.joeyreiman.com
www.dailyjoey.com
www.facebook.com/BrightHouse
www.twitter.com/BrightHouse

BIBLIOGRAPHY

"Bhutan GNH Index." Centre For Bhutan Studies & GNH Research. http://www.grossnational happiness.com/articles/.

Dicker, Ron. "Plastic Surgery Spending Is Up, As Number of Chin Augmentations Surges." *Huffington Post,* April 18, 2012. http://www .huffingtonpost.com/2012/04/18/plastic -surgery-spending-up-2011_n_1435512.html.

Kushner, Harold. *Who Needs God.* New York: Fireside, 2002.

OWN TV. "What Oprah Learned from Jim Carrey | Oprah's Lifeclass | Oprah Winfrey Network." YouTube video, 3:49. October 13, 2011. https://www.youtube.com /watch?v=nPU5bjzLZX0.

Parrott, Les, and Leslie Parrott. *I Love You More: How Everyday Problems Can Strengthen a Marriage.* Grand Rapids, MI: Zondervan, 2005.

Pollack, Andrew. "Akio Morita, Co-Founder of Sony and Japanese Business Leader, Dies at 78." *The New York Times,* October 4, 1999. http://www.nytimes.com/1999/10/04 /business/akio-morita-co-founder-of-sony-and -japanese-business-leader-dies-at-78.html.

Reiman, Joey. "10 BlackBerry Commandments." *LittlePinkBook.com,* May 20, 2013. http://www .littlepinkbook.com/10-blackberry -commandments.

Rosin, Hanna. "Why We Cheat: Spouses in happy marriages have affairs. What are we all looking for?" *Slate.com*, March 27, 2014. http://www .slate.com/articles/double_x/doublex/2014/03 /esther_perel_on_affairs_spouses_in_happy _marriages_cheat_and_americans_don.html.

ACKNOWLEDGMENTS

A book is not created by an author but by an army of talent.

Leading this effort is my dear friend, book expert, and publicist, Robyn Spizman, who grasped this book and never let it go until it was right in your hands. I have worked with Robyn for decades and known her family for thirty years. I am a better author and person because of all of them.

Robyn's daughter, Ali, is my executive assistant at BrightHouse and single-handedly coordinated all the hands that had a hand in creating *Thumbs Up*. Ali is positive, purposeful, fearless, and an action hero whose kindness is endless. A special thanks to Robyn's parents, Phyllis and Honey, as well for their words of wisdom. And thank you to Evelyn Sacks for giving me multiple hours of her time that will last a lifetime.

My endless gratitude to my wife, soul mate, muse, and co-author of my life, Cynthia Good. She gave me her hand in marriage and provides love, solace, and *opthumbmism*—all the things this writer needed to create this book.

To our loving sons, Alden, a junior at Emory University, and Julien, a freshman at Washington University in St. Louis, thank you for giving Dad a thumbs up every day. As I wrote this book, I thought of you both carrying it into your lives and providing inspiration to others.

My dedicated literary agent, Jackie Meyer, has a company named Whimsy Literacy, and that is what she has provided me for three decades: a place to make my dreams a reality. Jackie, thank you for making it happen and making it possible.

Thanks to the brilliant BenBella team who has put their heart, soul, and warmth into this book: publisher Glenn Yeffeth; the Strategic Positioning & Packaging team, Adrienne Lang, Sarah Dombrowsky, and Alicia Kania; my amazing editor, Vy Tran; production associate Jessika Rieck; and senior marketing associate Cameron Proffitt.

Thank you to my colleagues at BrightHouse, especially our leadership, President Cathy Carlisi, Executive Vice President Dolly Meese, and Chief Financial Officer Kim Rich. Every day you help Fortune 500 companies give a thumbs up to the world. Special kudos to the BrightHouse design team, Jeff Harter and Pedro Iwamoto. And *obrigado* to BrightHouse Brasil and its leaders, Jamie and Cecelia Troiano.

To my Emory teaching assistants, especially Amanda Wikman, who is now a strategist at BrightHouse, thank you for giving me a helping hand while mine were at work. And to my students in IDEATION 441 at the Goizueta Business School, thank you for teaching me lifelong lessons.

A thumbs up to two of my mentors: Al Hampel, whose Thumbs Up mind-set set my mind for success, and Maynard Jackson, who, though he is gone from earth, will always live in my heart.

My victory finger points to the heavens for sending the South African minister to me years ago so that I might discover my purpose.

Deep thanks to Dr. Arthur Cohen, Dr. Randy Martin, Dr. Libby Tannenbaum, and Peter Risdon, who give me the courage to give my middle finger to fear. *Namaste* to my yoga instructor, Carly Grace Hinchman, owner of Thunderbolt Power Yoga in Atlanta, whose purpose is to lead people into the life they love.

To my anti-bummer squad: Jay and Arlene Gould, Cathy Carlisi and Joe Paprocki, Ashley and Alex Maiola, Craig and Amy Weil, Meg Reggie and Rick Butgereit, Robyn and Ed Gerson, Rilla DeLorier and Chuck Allen, Glenn and Debbie Maron, Albert and Maria Amato, Danika and David Lewis, and my trainers, Jeff Cervero and Angie Perry, who help me march forth every day.

Thanks to all my friends who prove with their love that little is the new big and that material things are immaterial. To my followers on Twitter who send me little notes—you make such a big difference in my day. Thank you, Scott Gaston, for your little miracles, and astrologers Lorelei Robbins and Susie Cox for a little help from the stars.

To my mother and father up there, thanks for sending down so many thumbs up in my life. And to my brother Michael, who has been dealt a very good hand—use it.

Writing *Thumbs Up* was an act of love, because what I love most in the world is empowering others. There is nothing greater than giving your hand to another.

This book is based on my first book, which inspired a father to give it to his son. The son took the work and made it his life's work. He is now the deputy editor of *Fast Company*. Congratulations to you, David Lidsky, and God bless your dad. And to Dr. Marianne Garber and Robyn Spizman, who gave me a hand with the edits that brought that first book to life, many thanks. Which brings me full circle to the one I thank for everything—

Thank God for God.

ABOUT THE AUTHOR

Named "one of the 100 people who will change the way the world thinks" by *Fast Company*, Joey Reiman is CEO and founder of the International Center for Applied Purpose and the global consultancy Bright-House, a company whose mission is to bring greater purpose to the world of business.

Father of ideation—a term he coined—Reiman has emerged as the subject matter expert in the area of purpose, inspired leadership, marketing, and innovation.

His breakthrough purpose methodology and frameworks have been adopted by the likes of Procter & Gamble, The Coca-Cola Company, McDonald's, American Express, KPMG, American Standard, and many other Fortune 500 companies across the globe.

As an adjunct professor at the Goizueta School of Business at Emory University, he teaches tomorrow's executives his revolutionary theories and applications for purpose-inspired profit.

Reiman's breakthrough book, *The Story of Purpose: The Path to Creating a Brighter Brand, a Greater*

Company, and a Lasting Legacy, follows in the tradition of his wildly selling business book, *Thinking For A Living,* and has been named by the Raleigh, NC *News & Observer* as one of the top twenty-five books for corporate America.

Reiman is a frequent marketing and branding guest expert on CNN and is a monthly columnist for *BE* magazine, created by Mahatma Gandhi's grandson, Arun Gandhi. World-renowned Professor Philip Kotler calls Reiman "the Moses of Marketing." Winner of hundreds of awards, including the Cannes Lion and Corporate Marketing Leader of the Year, Reiman says his greatest accolade is his self-proclaimed title of FAMILLIONAIRE—a person whose real wealth is in his family.